Parkstone-on-Sea

Salterns, Sandbanks & Seaplanes

by

Jeremy Waters

This volume is published by the Poole Historical Trust whose primary aims are the promotion of research into and the publication of works on the history and life of Poole and the surrounding area.

Previous Publications

The Pride of Poole, 1688-1851
An Album of Old Poole
Mansions and Merchants of Poole and Dorset
Brownsea Islander
Poole and World War II
A Portfolio of Old Poole
Ebb-Tide at Poole
History of the Town of Poole, 1839 (facsimile)
The Sydenhams of Poole (booklet)
Art in Poole and Dorset
Victorian Poole
Poole after World War II 1945-1953
D-Day Poole (booklet)
The Spirit of Poole 1953-1963
Lifeboatmen Never Turn Back
Schools of Old Poole
Poole's Pride Regained 1964-1974
Poole Was My Oyster
Hengistbury Head - The Whole Story
I Was There
For Nature Not Humans
The Royal Motor Yacht Club 1905-2005 (private publication)
A Winsome Place
A Pint of Good Poole Ale
Up On Hill
Brownsea Island (facsimile of Van Raalte 1906)
Book of Poole High Street
Book of Poole Quay and the Waterfront

ISBN 978 - 1 - 873535 - 899
Production by Graphic Editions Ltd, Poole. Printed by Ashley Press, Poole, Dorset.

Acknowledgements & Thanks

I never intended to write a book. Indeed, if I had known what hard work it was going to be, I might never have attempted it. When I started research into the history of the Blue Lagoon, some ten years ago, it was just to satisfy my own curiosity, because I lived nearby. Then, having found out lots of stuff which I thought was interesting, I put together an illustrated talk to share it with others; they too thought it was interesting, and things snowballed. I would be surprised if there are now many fellowship organisations within ten miles on whom I have not inflicted a talk. Regularly I have been asked by members of my audience "Have you written a book?". So now I have.

This research has been carried out over several years, and has taken me to a wide range of archives. Lots of local people have been a huge help to me with their memories, photos and memorabilia. I am most grateful to them all and, if I have failed to acknowledge anyone's contribution, I apologise most sincerely.

I owe a particular debt to Aimee Alexander of Poole Flying Boats Celebration for sharing her knowledge of flying boats and the war years; to Andrew Hawkes who has given me both advice and generous access to his unrivalled collection of historic photographs of Poole; to the Harbour Commissioners, who allowed me to research historic Minute Books and ancient charts; and to all the staff at the Local Studies Centre at Poole Museum and the Dorset History Centre in Dorchester, who have proved both knowledgeable and unfailingly helpful. More local people should be made aware what a wonderful resource is available in these last two locations.

Amongst others who have helped me are Frank Ahern of Canford School Archives with data on Canford Manor, Jean Aish with Land Registry records, Elizabeth Bloxham of Canford School, Peter Burt of the Royal Motor Yacht Club, Peter Dobson of the Elms Estate Residents Association, Frank Henson who contributed numerous photos and historic newspapers, Jenny Oliver, Jamie Pride of Canford Cliffs Land Society, John Smith of Salterns Marina, and Gerry Wareham and his colleagues at Poole Maritime Trust. Colin Stone, who knows everything about local railways, always found time to help, as did Andrew Philpott who has a wide knowledge of the houses on Sandbanks.

I am most grateful to Pat Allen, Jon Hooker, Georgina Stanley, Vivienne St.Clair, Vernon Woodford and Anthony Yeatman, who all gave me access to elements of their family histories. I hope they will feel that I have treated their ancestors fairly. Others who have shared research, memories or photographs with me include Bertie Bowman, Mary Cooper, Tom Denley, Annelise Fielding, the Rev. Peter Huxham, Sir John James, Ken Latham, Tom Moore, Ken Oxford, Martin Pitts Crick, Babs Plumbridge, Valerie Sheldon, Jo Wallace-Smith and David Williams. I thank them all.

I have included a number of pre-war aerial photographs gathered from a variety of sources including the Local Studies Centre, my postcard collection and from pictures borrowed from neighbours' walls; although they are not so marked, it is likely that most of these were taken originally by Aerofilms. Their archive of negatives has been acquired by English Heritage who are gradually digitising them and making them available on their website 'Britain from Above'. They have not yet posted any that I have used, but I look forward to seeing their better quality pictures in due course.

I have also included numerous extracts from historic maps, including those published by H. M. Ordnance Survey, available in the libraries of Poole Local Studies Centre and Dorset History Centre. These are now well over 50 years old and outside their copyright period, but I acknowledge my debt to them, and my appreciation of the skills of those who produced them.

Although I like to think that this book approaches its subject from a slightly different viewpoint from previous authors, I readily admit to having plundered the works of others for background relating to my area of study. These include John Sydenham's "History of the Town and County of Poole" published in 1839, the many excellent publications of Poole Historical Trust and the "Looking Back..." series by Iris Morris. I have also referred to the interesting histories of Parkstone Yacht Club, Parkstone Golf Club, Lilliput Sailing Club, the Royal Motor Yacht Club, Conifer Park and Canford Manor.

Approximately half the illustrations included in this book are from my own collection, but the balance have been contributed by others, to whom I am extremely grateful. Without their help, there would be no book. Specifically they include Andrew Hawkes' Poole Picture Archive [illustrations numbered 11, 15, 18, 19, 26, 43, 45, 56, 57, 59, 60, 62, 64, 65, 68, 71, 76, 77, 81, 85, 88, 89, 100, 111, 127, 129, 141, 142, 143, 148, 149, 152, 153, 154, 161,163, 166, 171, 172, 176, 181, 188, 204, 205 & 262]; the Andreae Family [130 &131], Canford Cliffs Land Society [144,145, & 147], Canford School Archive [7 & 116], Colin Stone [22, 40, 41 & 184], David Williams [198], Dorset History Centre [20 & 21], Dorset Life Magazine [160], Frank Henson [58, 91, 119, 135, 185 & 186], Gordon Cousins [178 & 206], Imperial War Museum [213, 215 & 222], Jon Hooker [128], Ken Latham [52], Kitchenham Photography [267 & cover photo], Leslie Dawson [233] Lilliput Sailing Club [264], Michael Tombs [160], Mary Cooper [207], Parkstone Yacht Club [118], Peter Dobson [53], Poole Flying Boats Celebration [208, 209, 212, 214, 216, 217, 218, 219, 220, 221, 225, 226, 228, 229, 231, 232, 239, 240, 241, 249 & 265]; Poole Local Studies Centre [1, 3, 5, 9, 10, 12, 13, 14, 17, 25, 27, 28, 31, 35, 36, 38, 39, 42, 44, 50, 51, 80, 113, 115, 150, 151, 156, 167, 173, 174, 190, 191, 194, 199, 201, 203, 210, 250 & 257], Ronald Pitts Crick [235 & 237], Poole Historical Trust [6, 8, 82, 211, 243, 244, 245, 246, 247, 248 & 252], Royal Motor Yacht Club [136, 139, 236, 238 & 242], Salterns Marina [258], St. Luke's Church, Parkstone [74], Valerie Sheldon [84], Vivien Farquharson [124] and the Woodford Family [195].

Every effort has been made to trace the owners of any original material reproduced in this book, and should it contain any pictures which are still in copyright to the original photographer, I apologise and would be grateful to be told about them.

I have very much appreciated the help and guidance of my Publisher, Poole Historical Trust, and its Hon. Secretary, Ian Andrews. If there are any mistakes of fact, they are mine alone, and if any reader can offer any corrections, suggestions or comments, I would welcome hearing from them at jeremy.waters5@btinternet.com.

Contents

Introduction

The northern shore of Poole Harbour, from the harbour entrance to the edge of Poole Park, was often referred to by the Victorians as "Parkstone-on-Sea". Today it is an exclusively residential area, including some of the most expensive houses in the country. Yet it hasn't always been like that. For most of recorded history, Parkstone's main justification has been industry. There was the mining and manufacture of alum and copperas; commercial salt manufacturing; pottery-making on an industrial scale; heavy engineering with a railway to a shipping wharf; numerous boat-building yards; a seaplane training school and a flying boat base which, for almost ten years, transformed the harbour into the country's principal international airport.

Whether smuggling counts as an industry may be debateable, but that too was widespread in the eighteenth and nineteenth centuries, when Isaac Gulliver and other 'free traders' brought in contraband through the chines of Poole and Bournemouth and across the open heath beyond.

As we take modern transport for granted, it becomes difficult to remember quite how much this has shrunk the areas in which we live. Today it takes little more than 10 minutes to whisk in our cars over metalled roads along the five miles from central Poole to the tip of Sandbanks. A century and a half ago, on foot, over unmade tracks, this was a much more significant journey, and what now seems to be one continuous residential sprawl was originally several distinct settlements with open fields or woods between them. In this book, I will try to give you just a taste of the history of the areas we now know as Sandbanks, Lilliput, Whitecliff, and Ashley Cross, even touching on Canford Cliffs, including many of the long-forgotten commercial activities which were so important to the prosperity of those who lived here.

I trained as a Chartered Surveyor in Bournemouth in the 1950s, but spent most of my working life in London. When I retired back home to Poole, and found a house with a frontage to the muddy waters of what is now called "the Blue Lagoon" in Lilliput, I was intrigued by the origins of this shallow backwater. This started me on many enjoyable years of research into the local history of the area. Much of this was based on the rich legacy of maps and charts, stretching back more than 500 years, available in local archives. These make it clear how much Parkstone has changed, particularly over the past century. This book is my attempt to record what it used to be like.

This book is by no means all original research, but pulls together data from many sources relating to the lovely part of Poole in which I live. I cannot claim it to be a comprehensive history, but I hope it tells you something you didn't already know, and that you enjoy sharing what I have discovered.

Jeremy Waters. 2014.

1. The approximate extent of the Estate of Canford Manor at the beginning of the 19th century. The western boundary is the most difficult to identify with certainty, but the others are clear. The eastern boundary originally ran to the mouth of the Bourne stream, but by this time the West Cliff had been sold to the Dean family.

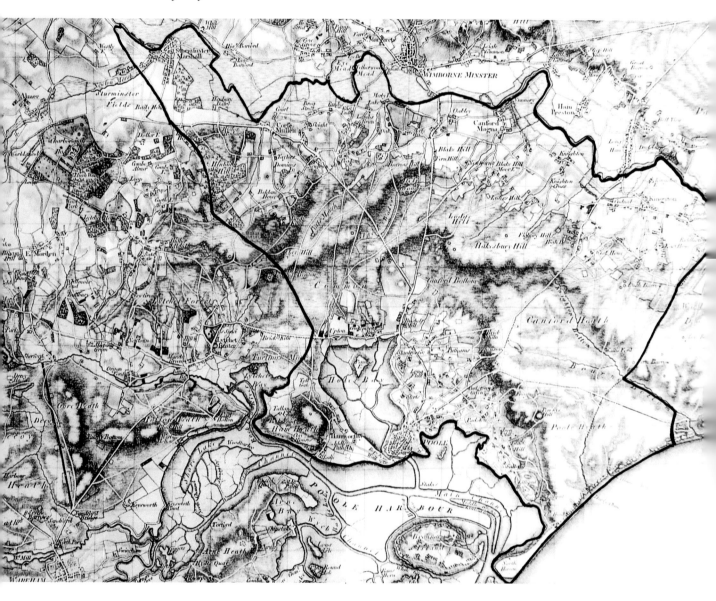

Chapter 1:

Canford Manor and 'The Mynes'

Parkstone lies at the southern edge of Canford Manor. This huge estate, dating from Norman times, was originally bordered in the south by the shore of Poole Harbour, from its inner reaches at Rockley to the harbour entrance and along the sea shore as far as the mouth of the Bourne. Its eastern boundary followed the Bourne stream as far as Coy Pond and then turned north to Kinson along an ancient trackway following the county boundary. In the north it followed the River Stour to Wimborne. The western boundary is less clear because it crossed virtually featureless heathland, but early records suggest it followed part of the Roman road from Hamworthy to Badbury Rings. In total, it originally extended to something over 17,000 acres.

The manor house, now Canford School, was largely rebuilt in the 1850s, but the estate was listed in the Domesday Book, which records that *Edward of Salisbury holds Canford from the King*. It has had many noble owners in the subsequent thousand years, perhaps the most romantic of which is the gallant medieval knight, William Longesword II

2. Canford Manor was much photographed for local postcards, as this picture from about 1905 testifies.

who granted Poole its first Charter in 1248. This cost the town the huge sum of 70 marks, which helped to fund the knight's crusade to the Holy Land where he met his death in battle.

As with many estates which were granted by the Crown to those who had served it well, the grant could equally be revoked if the King were displeased. It seems that this did occur on several occasions, from the 14th to the 17th century, when Canford reverted to the Crown, and was then granted afresh to a new favourite.

The main house is located at Canford Magna, on the northern boundary of the estate, amongst the best farmland and on an attractive site by the River Stour. Most of the southern part of the estate, that part which became known as Parkstone was, until the 19th century, mainly heathland: open unfenced common land, of little use for anything but rough grazing for pigs and cattle, and cutting turf for burning. Although there were some small areas of indigenous woodland on the lower slopes around the harbour edge, it was not until the early 19th century that the planting of pine trees that characterised Canford Cliffs and Branksome Park in particular was carried out.

Most authorities agree that the most likely derivation of the name 'Parkstone' was

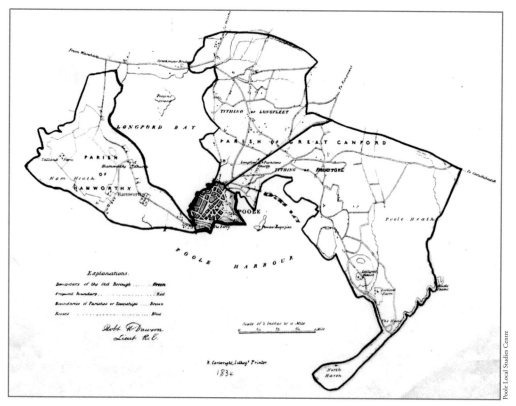

3. A map dated 1834 in the Poole Local Studies Centre which shows the boundaries of Poole Old Town and how the Borough was extended by the addition of Hamworthy, Longfleet and Parkstone. This makes it clear that the extent of the original Tithing of Parkstone was very much larger than the area that we think of as Parkstone today.

from a stone marking the boundary of a deer park belonging to Canford Manor – venison was then an important source of food for the ruling classes. There are references in early documents to Parkeston in 1326, Parkestone in 1494, Parkston in 1586 and Parkson in 1774, and today's spelling of Parkstone is standard by about 1850. It became an ecclesiastical parish, independent of Canford Magna, with the establishment of St. Peter's Church at Ashley Cross in 1833, and in 1835 the boundaries of the Borough of Poole were extended to take in Parkstone, together with Longfleet and Hamworthy.

Many will be surprised that a county as rural as Dorset can claim to be the birthplace of a major industry, but it is a realistic claim that Parkstone was the place where the chemical industry first started in this country. The manufacture of alum and copperas from raw mineral soils available in the area represented a major change from other local industries of the medieval period, in that it involved continuously-operated chemical processes over several years. It therefore required considerable planning, financial investment and infrastructure.

It is clear from the accounts of the Reeve of Canford Manor that 'alome' had been discovered on the estate early in the 16th century. Alum and copperas were, at this time, two of the most important commodities traded in Europe. Alum was used as a mordant or fixative in the dyeing of cloth, and for the tanning and softening of leather. Copperas was also used as a mordant, as well as a black dye and in the manufacture of ink. They also had uses locally as a treatment of infection in the feet of the many sheep on which much of Dorset's livelihood depended. Above all, alum was used as a purifying agent in the manufacture of saltpetre, a major component of gunpowder. The main sources of supply were from the Papal states of Italy, which exercised control over both supply and price, so the English Crown began actively to encourage the investigation of domestic sources by granting patents to those prepared to undertake the exploration and manufacture of these minerals.

It was in the middle of the 16th century, at a time when the Manor had a rapid succession of owners, that Parkstone first comes to prominence. In 1536 Henry VIII conferred the Manor on Henry Courteney, Marquis of Exeter, jointly with his wife Gertrude. However, three years later, the Marquis was executed for high treason and the Manor reverted to the Crown. In 1547, following the accession of the young king Edward VI, it was granted to Edward Seymour, Duke of Somerset, but when he too was executed for treason in 1552, it again reverted to the Crown. In 1553, when Queen Mary came to the throne, she returned Canford Manor to Gertrude, the widowed Marchioness of Exeter who eventually bequeathed two-thirds of the estate to her nephew, James Blount, the 6th Lord Mountjoy in 1558.

James Blount (pronounced 'Blunt') was aged only 24 when he inherited Canford Manor. Although from a very well-connected family, he was already heavily in debt due to his lavish lifestyle, costly military service and law suits over his inheritance. Described by one source as *"financially reckless and doubtfully honest"*, he was immediately obliged to mortgage both Canford and the Manor of Puddletown which came to him at the same time. He was, however, something of a scientist, described as a *"curious searcher into nature"*, and *"a confirmed dabbler in alchemy"*. Aware of their potential, he saw the minerals on Canford Manor as a way to restore his fortune.

Mountjoy was aware that, since about 1535, deposits of alum-bearing earth had been discovered in Parkstone, particularly on the cliffs where it had become exposed by natural erosion. From this raw material could be manufactured the valuable alum and copperas, although the actual process of manufacture was little known outside Italy, and much experimentation was needed to achieve the desired result. There was also the problem that all mineral rights belonged to the Crown. His opportunity came when, in 1566, Queen Elizabeth granted a patent to a Cornelius de Vos of Liege for 21 years, to open and work mines anywhere in England for the production of copperas and

4. James Blount, Lord Mountjoy.

5. Extract from Christopher Saxton's map of Dorset, published in 1575, marking "The Mynes" at or around Lilliput, and "Canford Lawndes", i.e. Canford Heath.

Poole Local Studies Centre

alum. Encouraged by a family friend, Lord William Cecil, Secretary of State to the Queen, Mountjoy negotiated an assignment of the patent and immediately invested heavily in mining and manufacturing facilities in Parkstone, employing Cornelius Stephinsonn as his manager.

Today the exact location of Mountjoy's alum and copperas 'houses' is no longer clear. Early records tell us that the first two of these were located on "Canford Launds" and at "Okeman's House"; the latter is likely have to have been on or close to Okeman's Hill, today known as Evening Hill at Lilliput, although another suggestion is that it could be by the lagoon at Salterns. The general location is confirmed by early maps of Dorset – like that by Christopher Saxton - which mark, on or around Lilliput, "The Mynes". Other early maps describe the land to the east of Canford Cliffs Chine as "Mines Common" or "Mines Heath". Certainly Mountjoy built a copperas house at Alum Chine, another at "Haven House" and also leased land on Brownsea Island to build another there.

The Port Books in the latter part of the 16th century show that large amounts of copperas and some alum were shipped out of Poole, bound mainly for London, Southampton and Holland. However, Mountjoy's venture was not the financial success for which he was hoping, almost certainly because the manufacturing processes to refine the chemicals from the raw earth proved too lengthy and expensive. Nevertheless, it is fair to regard Mountjoy's endeavours as the very start of the chemical manufacturing industry in this country – the fore-runner of ICI!

As Mountjoy's financial situation grew more desperate, in 1568 he attempted to safeguard the future of his wife, Catherine, and five children, by placing the works at Okeman's House in trust for them, administered by four trustees. The venture continued to make a loss and eventually in 1570, pressed by his creditors, Mountjoy sold off most of the Manor to Henry Hastings, 3rd Earl of Huntingdon, another of the great Elizabethan courtiers.

Huntingdon also hoped he might add to his fortune by operating the alum and copperas mines. However it appears that, in the small print of the conveyance, Mountjoy had kept the mining rights for himself, and a long and bitter legal action followed. This was exacerbated by an attempt by Mountjoy's sons, following his death in 1581, to lease the works at Okeman's House to Edward Meade, which Lord Huntingdon considered was encroaching on his manorial rights.

The bitter legal proceedings were not settled until 1586, long after Mountjoy's death. The Privy Council then ruled that the Earl of Huntingdon was the rightful owner of Canford Manor, including the mining rights, but that he was required to make a payment of £6,000 in compensation to Mountjoy's son, William. Mining continued throughout the period of the legal dispute, the works being leased to various operators but, despite the investment of more than £20,000 in legal fees and development costs, neither the 3rd Earl, nor his successors, was able to make the venture really profitable. It seems that manufacturing petered out soon after 1600, and the works at Parkstone fell into decay.

In 1608, the 5th Earl made an attempt to re-open the copperas works on Canford Manor. To provide the large amounts of turf needed to fire the manufacturing process, he started to fence off extensive areas of heathland around Parkstone. This had, since time immemorial, been common land on which the people of the Manor had grazed their cattle and cut turf for their fires, and the enclosures caused an uproar. Poole Borough Council started legal proceedings, and the Earl filed a Bill in Chancery in an attempt to make his actions lawful, but this was thrown out. Eventually he quietly backed down.

The Huntingdons held Canford Manor until 1611, when it was sold to Sir John Webb, a successful Roman Catholic merchant from Salisbury, who had been knighted in 1603 and wanted a family seat to match his new status. However, for reasons unknown, the Crown laid claim to the estate in 1628, and Charles I became Lord of the Manor until 1635 when it was returned to John Webb Esquire, the son of the earlier purchaser. The Webb family and its descendants then continued to own it for the next two centuries, putting their own mark on Parkstone by developing a commercial salt-making industry.

The oldest map of Canford Manor dates from the early 17th century and is now held in the Dorset History Centre in Dorchester. It is entitled "Canford Launnes. Mr Weeb his Lande", and was probably commissioned soon after 1635, when John Webb Esq. was granted Canford Manor by King Charles. It shows one of the earliest plans of Poole town, then almost entirely surrounded by water. The only approach from the mainland was guarded by the fortified Town Gate, located about where the train station is today.

To the north of the map, the land around the Manor House and the village of Canford Magna is shown in some detail, with the names of many occupiers given (including a previous

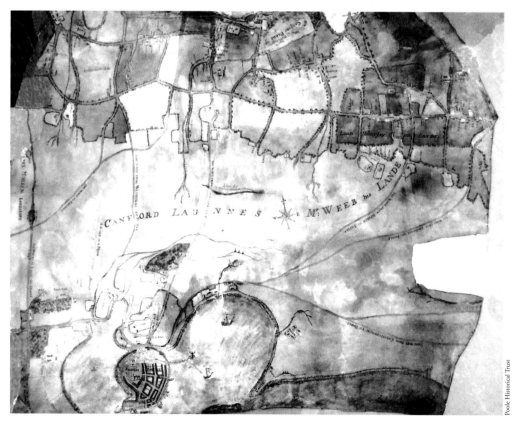

6. The "Canford Launnes" map of Canford Manor, dating from the early 1600s.

7. Sir Ivor Guest (1835-1914), First Baron Wimborne.

Canford School Archive

owner, Lord Mountjoy, who apparently still retained some land). However, the southern half of the Manor is shown virtually blank, marked as "Canford Launnes"; these lawns represented the barren heathland which then stretched uninterrupted, way beyond the boundaries of the Manor, as far as Christchurch and Ringwood.

The last family to own the Manor before it became a school was the Guests. The Welsh steel magnate, Sir John Guest, bought the remaining 13,000 acres of the estate in 1847 for £335,000. Persuaded to do so by his wife, Lady Charlotte, who hoped that the clean air would improve his health, Sir John was the immensely wealthy and hard-working owner of the great iron works in Dowlais, South Wales, which made many of the rails for the fast expanding railway networks around the world. He immediately commissioned Sir Charles Barry, the architect of the Houses of Parliament, to carry out extensive modifications, including the construction of the Great Hall, Library and tower, and it was not until these were completed that the family moved in to Canford. Sadly Sir John was to enjoy it for only two years before his death in 1852, when it was inherited by his 17 years old son Ivor, who was still at Cambridge.

Sir Ivor assumed the Lordship of the Manor when he became 21, but it was not until some years later when he married Lady Cornelia Churchill in 1868 that they went to live at Canford and he really took his responsibilities seriously. The couple became very popular amongst their tenants and the people of Poole, and were much involved in many of the projects to build new churches, public buildings and golf courses. Their largest gift was the land on which Poole Park was constructed. Sir Ivor was created Baron Wimborne of Canford Magna in 1880 in Disraeli's resignation honours list.

It is clear that, over the last 500 years, the Lords of the Manor of Canford have played a large part in the development of Parkstone, although much of this has been by exploiting the area's natural resources, whether minerals, salt, clay or building land. This process continued into the 19th and 20th centuries as land was sold off for residential development. It seems that the Manor was prepared to dispose of anything that lay outside the core agricultural holding at Wimborne, if the price was right. The Tithe Maps of Parkstone in the 1840s show that, although the Manor is still the major landowner, quite substantial areas had already been sold for farming or development. This is further illustrated by an Estate Map, based on the Ordnance Survey from just after 1900, which is coloured to show what land was still owned at that time and what had been sold. The northern part of the estate still formed a cohesive whole, but the south, from Poole to Branksome Park, showed a patchwork of sales. The major developments which resulted from these disposals will be considered in the following chapters.

8. Extract from the Canford Launnes map of around 1630, showing one of the earliest representations of Poole Town and the northern shore of the harbour. Parkson is marked, and the only other settlement shown is a cluster of buildings around Haven House, next to the Luscombe stream.

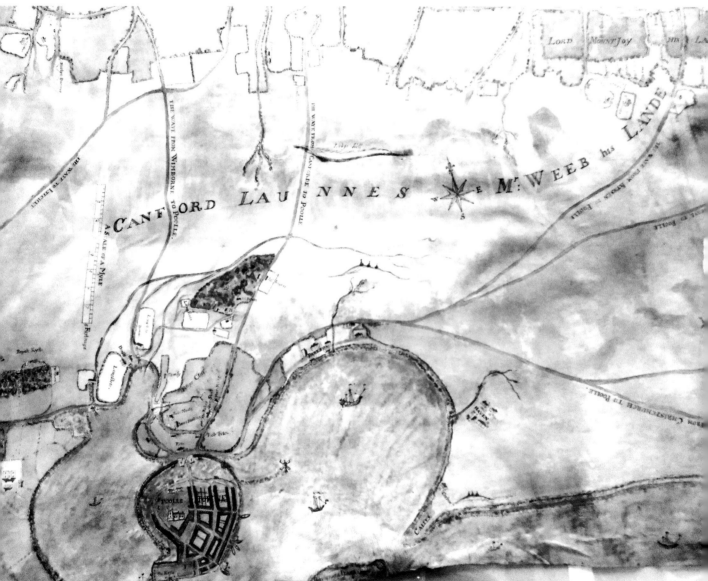

Chapter 2:

The Early Growth
of Parkson

Many of the estate records for Canford Manor were stored in London during the Second World War and were destroyed by bombing. Much of what remains is apparently located at Ashby St. Ledgers in Northamptonshire, the seat of the current Viscount Wimborne, but is neither catalogued nor accessible. As a result, limited sources remain to show how Parkstone developed. Fortunately, however, local archives hold a series of both charts of the harbour and maps of the area stretching back almost 500 years. There are also a few authoritative written sources, including "The History of the Town and County of Poole" by John Sydenham, first published in 1839 and reprinted by Poole Historical Trust in 1986. These sources allow us to see how Parkstone gradually developed amongst the low-lying woods and fields bordering the northern shore of Poole Harbour. The higher ground of Canford Heath, stretching inland and to the east, remained barren heathland until the founding of Bournemouth in the 19th century encouraged further development.

One of the oldest of the maps, dating from the about the 1630s, is the "Canford Launnes" map mentioned in the previous chapter. Although the mapmaker did not have the skills of later surveyors, Poole and Parkstone are readily identifiable, and it is clear that there was very little development outside the boundaries of Poole town itself.

The only settlements shown around the harbour shore are a small hamlet at "Parkson", another group of buildings at "Haven" next to the Luscombe stream, and a house belonging to W Corben, close to the neck of the sandbanks. No indication is given that any of the land was being farmed, or being used for any other purposes.

The Haven was undoubtedly one of the very first houses in Parkstone-on-Sea, situated at the bottom of Evening Hill, facing the harbour. It has been marked on maps with a variety of names over the centuries, initially as North Haven, Haven House or Haven Farm, then later as Lilliput Farm and, in the 20th century, Flag Farm. This map confirms that it was already in existence in the early 1600s. The sandbanks are inscribed with the old-fashioned name of "calles".

More than a century after the Canford Launnes map, Sir Peter Thompson, a native of Poole who had become a successful merchant in Bermondsey and High Sheriff of Surrey, commissioned a gift for the people of his home town: a new survey of the Harbour. Although primarily intended for maritime use, this early chart identifies a number of land-based features, including Haven House, and describes a large area of the Parkson shore as "corn lands". By this time, it seems clear that some of the land close to the harbour shore was gradually being turned to cultivation. The lagoon is named on this and on several other early charts as "Little Sea".

In 1763 Sir Peter Thompson decided *"to withdraw from the engagements of commercial affairs, that he might enjoy the pleasures of studious retirement and reflection, and the conversation*

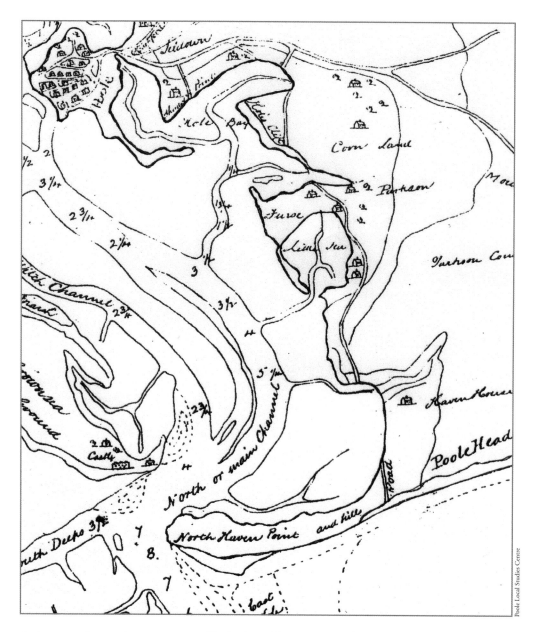

9. An extract from a chart commissioned by Sir Peter Thompson in 1745 as a gift to his home town of Poole. It is clear that the land along the northern shore of the harbour is now being turned to agricultural use.

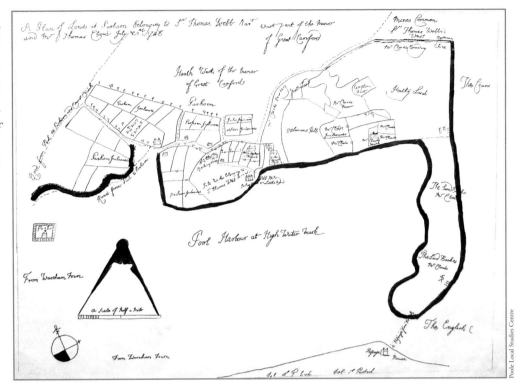

Poole Local Studies Centre

10. Map of Parkson dated July 2nd 1748, showing the respective ownerships of Sir Thomas Webb, Baronet, the Lord of the Manor of Canford, and of Mr Thomas Cload, owner of the Haven Estate.

of friends, in the place of his birth". He lived until his death in 1770 in the large and elegant house he built in Market Street, which is still there today, and a fine monument to him and other members of his family can be seen in St. James' Church in the Old Town of Poole.

Soon after Sir Peter Thompson's chart was published, the next map, now in Poole Museum, was prepared, for reasons which will be explained later. This is dated "July 20th 1748" and entitled *"A plan of lands at Parkson belonging to Sir Thomas Webb Baronet and Mr Thomas Cload".* It covers almost the whole of Parkstone-on-Sea, from today's Whitecliff in the west, to North Haven Point at the harbour entrance, and along the coast to Canford Cliffs Chine in the east.

This map confirms the location of the second of Parkstone's major industries, the salt works and boiling houses at Salterns belonging to the Lord of the Manor, Sir Thomas Webb. To the west of these is what is later to be known as the Elms Estate and to the east is Haven House, described as *"Mr Cloads House".* Along the harbour shore, numerous fields (inclosures) are shown, with farm houses and cottages for their workers. These, however, do not extend far inland, where the land is described as the *"heath wastes of the Manor of Great Canford".*

It is interesting to note that, amongst the names given to various areas of land on this map, *"Compton Acre"* was a separate enclosure more than 250 years ago. Beyond Bettmans Chine (now Canford Cliffs Chine), the land is described as *"Mines Common",* probably a reference to Mountjoy's alum mines.

The professional mapmaker and engraver, Isaac Taylor, published the first complete map of the County of Dorset in 1765. Although to a relatively small scale, the representation of the northern shore of the harbour is more accurately drawn and much more detailed than previous maps. The road from Poole town to the salterns is shown, as is the hamlet of Parkson. It marks *Parkson Mill*, which has been shown on earlier maps back as far as 1675, although on the 1811 Ordnance Survey it is described as an Iron Mill; the Tithe Map of 1844 shows it as a 'mill and mill-pond', so it was undoubtedly a water-mill. No trace of it remains, except that Mill Lane is still there to this day.

Taylor's map shows a *"Salt Office"* by the salterns, and *"North Haven"* (House) is clearly marked. The sandbanks are labelled as *"Sand Hills"*, and a *"Battery"* is shown as being sited under the cliff known as Poole Head, and another close to the harbour mouth. These would seem likely to be defensive installations with guns because, only a few years later, the wealthy Poole merchant, Isaac Lester, notes in his diary for 26th May 1778 that he sent men for *"the fixing of platforms for guns at Brownsea and Haven"*.

Many place names have changed over the centuries: on all the early maps and charts until the beginning of the 19th century, what we now call Parkstone Bay was called Holes Bay, and what we now know as Holes Bay has been given a variety of names including Longford Bay, Longfleet Bay and the Harbour Pool. Sandbanks Road was, until a century ago, known as Salterns Road, simply because the salterns were the most important place in Parkstone until salt production ended in the early 1800s. Lilliput has moved from what we now call Evening Hill to absorb Salterns – in the late 1800s the local paper carried a number of indignant letters from residents in the Salterns area, complaining that the upstart Lilliput was becoming confused with their much older location. But even before Evening Hill became known as Lilliput, it is marked on early maps as "Oakmans Hill".

Inevitably, map-makers sometimes just get names wrong, either misheard from a local resident with a broad dialect, or incorrectly engraved. This may well account for the first known reference to Lilliput, which is on the earliest maritime chart of the harbour produced by the Hydrographical Office in 1785, which looks as though it is spelled *"Elipute"*. In all later charts, and on maps prepared by the Ordnance Survey, it is corrected to *"Lilliput"*.

That first Admiralty chart (see fig. 12) comes twenty years after Isaac Taylor's map. It marks a *"Salt House"* by the edge of the lagoon, where the seawater was boiled to produce salt, and it now shows a brick kiln on the Elms Estate. A new *"Summer House"* (the first Lilliput House) is shown on the bluff, high up on Evening Hill, undoubtedly marked on this maritime chart because it was a prominent landmark for incoming shipping. Another landmark, a *"Flagstaff"*, is marked at the location of Haven House, where a Coastguard Station was maintained, and this almost certainly is the reason the farm later became known as "Flag Farm".

The most accurate of all the early maps is the very first Ordnance Survey of Poole, published on 10th April 1811, which shows a district which is becoming clearly recognisable as the Parkstone of today.

The French Revolution of 1789 had caused great unease in British government circles, further increased by the rise to power of Napoleon at the turn of the century. The threat of war with France and the possibility of invasion meant accurate maps were essential, and a military-led survey of the South Coast started in 1794. After the initial triangulation,

11. Extract from Isaac Taylor's map of the County of Dorsetshire, published in 1765.

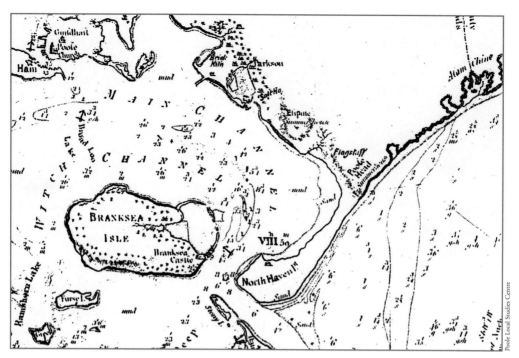

12. Extract from the first maritime chart of Poole Harbour prepared by the Admiralty's Hydrographical Office in 1785, identifying landmarks such as the brick kiln on the Elms peninsular and a 'Summer House' on the site of today's Lilliput House on Evening Hill.

the detailed topography of the area from Christchurch to Wareham was filled in by the surveyors between 1801 and 1805, and their field notes were then taken to their offices in the Tower of London to be engraved onto metal plates before eventual publication. This map therefore is quite the best record available of the situation on the ground in Parkstone and the surrounding area in the first few years of the 19th century.

This 1811 Ordnance Survey map makes it very clear how little development there was in Parkstone only 200 years ago. Poole itself is now less of an island because land has been gradually reclaimed, and development has expanded beyond its medieval gates into Longfleet. However, to the east, beyond the scattered settlements along the harbour shore, there was absolutely nothing but wild heath as far as the mouth of the Bourne stream – where Lewis Tregonwell was building the very first house in Bournemouth in the very year this map was published. Indeed, that heathland stretched virtually uninterrupted as far as Christchurch and Ringwood.

Looking at the OS map, it is easy to see why the name 'Parkstone-on-Sea' arose: all the early development has taken place amongst the fields and woods along the harbour shore. The roads, which were originally just footpaths to gain access to cottages and fields, are by now becoming more clearly defined, and "Parkston Green" consists of a few houses around a crossroads on the road from Poole to Christchurch. This road had been adopted by Poole's Turnpike Trust in 1810 and improved to a standard which would accept wheeled vehicles, although tolls were charged as a consequence. What we know today as Blake Hill is marked

13. Extract from the first Ordnance Survey map of East Dorset, published in 1811.

on the map as "Black Hill" and Penn Hill is called "Penny's Hill". Three houses are named individually – "Salterns", "Lilliput House" and "Lilliput Farm". The only building of any kind on the sandbanks is the Coastguard Station.

Parkstone's industry is clearly illustrated: the "Parkson Mill" shown on Isaac Taylor's map of 1765 is now described as an "Iron Mill", which we know made sharp-edged tools. The salt pans and the boiling houses of Canford Manor's salt-works are still a major feature, although these are to fall into disuse within about 20 years.

Throughout the 18th century, Parkstone Village was just a hamlet situated a pleasant mile and a half's walk through country lanes outside Poole, on the unmade road to Christchurch. Once travellers had passed through the village and climbed eastward up the hill onto the heath, the surroundings changed: the route was described in The Universal British Directory of 1798 as crossing *"a barren dreary heath which affords no pleasant views to travellers who come from the more delightful parts of the country"*. This opinion was confirmed by the Duke of Rutland, who published in 1805 his Journal of a Tour around the Southern Coasts of England, writing *"From Christchurch, we proceeded on horseback towards Poole...on the barren uncultivated heath where we were, there was not a human being to direct us"*.

The Early Growth of Parkson

The mapmakers, C & J Greenwood carried out a detailed survey of Dorset between 1826 and 1827, and their map illustrates how Parkstone was beginning to evolve as a distinct community. There is increasing residential development centred around today's Ashley Cross where the Britannia Inn is marked, and extending up Castle Hill where Sandecotes Road and St. Osmunds Road now run southward. Sites here enjoyed extensive views out across the harbour and were starting to be developed with large houses on private estates, including Castle Eve and Sandecotes Manor. Sandy Lane, today's Canford Cliffs Road, is shown extending from Branksome through Penny's Hill to the harbour shore, but Western Avenue seems to wander off across Poole Heath towards a misplaced Durley Chine.

Greenwoods' map shows few changes from the first Ordnance Survey, except that they clearly show how much of the bare heathland, such as Branksome Park, was now being planted with pine trees. The Enclosure Acts at last enabled landowners to cultivate those areas of what had previously been common land; Canford's poor heathland was not suitable for farming, but would grow timber to generate long-term income and, following the end of the Napoleonic wars, there were many unemployed servicemen eager for work. The new neighbour, Bournemouth, had already planted many hundreds of thousands of pine trees by this stage. The other change shown on the Greenwoods' map is that Lilliput House is described as 'ruins'. This would have been the first house on the site; Lilliput House is still there in the same place today, but is a much later replacement building. The saltworks are no longer shown and most of the surrounding area still comprises small tenanted farms belonging to Canford Manor.

Poole's great historian, John Sydenham, gives a glowing account of Parkstone a few years later in 1839, describing it as: "a hamlet....in the parish of Great Canford ..... delightfully situated, and due to its scenic beauties, convenient distance from the town, and proximity to the sea, its population is rapidly increasing". Poole itself was not then a pleasant place in which to live. The prosperity created by the Newfoundland cod trade in the previous century had become a distant memory and the old town was now a crowded and impoverished place. Those who could afford it were happy to move out to new villas in more pleasant rural surroundings; many of these grew up around what we now call Ashley Cross, then Parkstone Green or Parkstone Village. This got its first pub, The Britannia Inn, in about 1825. This was soon to be followed by a church, the first St. Peters, built largely at the expense of the brothers, R.H and R.W Parr, and consecrated in October 1833 by the Bishop of Bath and Wells before a gathering of *all the respectability of the neighbourhood*. Parkstone then became a separate parish from Canford Magna. It also got its own postal service in 1834, operated from the main post Office in the town of Poole, although the postman's round extended as far as the Bath Hotel in Bourne.

Parkstone Village continued to grow throughout the second half of the 19th century and, although the saltworks had gone, there were still a number of brickworks, and soon another major industry was to come to the area which would shape its development for much of the next century. The sandbanks, meanwhile, were still considered wild and remote and, apart from the resident Coastguard, rarely visited by anyone except fishermen, wildfowlers and, almost certainly, by smugglers.

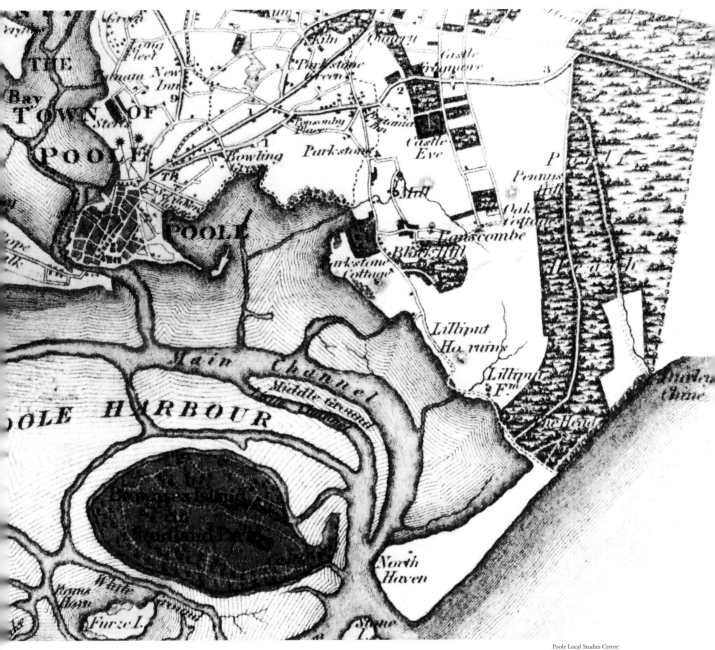

14. Extract from a map of Dorset published by Messrs C & J Greenwood from a survey carried out in the years 1826 – 1827. It shows the start of development around Castle Eve and Sandecotes, off the top of Castle Hill, and much new afforestation.

The Early Growth of Parkson

Andrew Hawkes' Poole Picture Archive

15. *Parr Street in Parkstone Village in about 1860, showing the first church of St Peter's, consecrated in 1833. As the population increased, there became a need for a larger building, which was constructed in stages between 1876 and 1901. On the left is the Church School, still to be seen today.*

16. *A poster from 1839 advertising the postal service now available in Parkstone and Bourne(mouth) through the good offices of the appropriately named postman, Charles Satchell. Bourne was not yet large enough to justify a post office of its own.*

PARKSTONE & BOURNE
POST OFFICE.

The Inhabitants of PARKSTONE and BOURNE are respectfully informed, that the Post Town appointed for the delivery of Letters for the above places, is POOLE; and that there is a Receiving House at PARKSTONE, which has been established five years; and that I, as the regularly appointed POSTMAN, deliver and receive the Post Letters at Parkstone, Bourne, and the immediate Neighbourhood, and call at the Bath Hotel, and the Tregonwell Arms, Bourne, every day.

CHARLES SATCHELL.

Parkstone, May 6, 1839.

J. R. JUSTICAN, PRINTER, HIGH STREET, POOLE.

Chapter 3:

The Haven Estate

In 1610, the year before the Webb family acquired Canford Manor, the 5th Earl of Huntingdon granted the most southerly part of the estate to a Nicholas Mead of Barkham, Berkshire. We know this area today as Evening Hill, Canford Cliffs and Sandbanks, but it was then called 'The Haven Estate'. For the next 150 years, the Haven Estate was to remain in separate ownership from the Manor, passing down from Nicholas Mead to his grand-daughter, Elizabeth Morris, and then to several generations of wealthy Poole sea captains called Cload.

The Mead family had been involved with Parkstone for many years: it was an attempt to lease Okeman's copperas house to an Edward Mead in 1581 which formed part of Lord Huntingdon's legal action against the Mountjoys. This Mead had incurred substantial expenditure of some £1700 on restoring the works and, as late as 1594, was still trying to recover the debt, petitioning that the late Lord and Lady Mountjoy had *"prevailed on him to set working their copperas works called Okeman's, Dorset, then utterly decayed"*. It is possible that the grant to Nicholas of the Haven Estate might have been part of the settlement of this debt. It could even be that the family had been tenants there, because yet a third Mead, Richard, is recorded as having been most viciously murdered only a few years earlier, in 1598, by *"three wicked men"* at Haven House.

The next reference to the estate is in an inventory held at The National Archives, made on 14th June 1671 listing *"all and singular the earthly goods, rights, credits and chattels of Thomas Cload of Haven neere Poole in the County of Dorset"*. Such inventories were usually made following a death and this one gives a picture of a very comfortably furnished home, as well as a well equipped farm with hogs, rams, 26 lambs, 14 sheep, *"16 acres of oats, barley, peas and rye, and 10 stocks of bees"*.

The separate ownership of the Haven Estate must have rankled with a much later lord of Canford Manor, Sir Thomas Webb, because he took legal action in the Court of Chancery in about 1745 to try to regain possession from the then owner, a Captain Thomas Cload. In his evidence to the court, Thomas Cload gave an account of his family's long ownership of the land, and explained that even the wild and uninhabited sandbanks (referred to using the archaic word 'cales') had a commercial value, for cutting rushes and for the right of wreck. One witness, Mary Barnes of Parkstone, whose mother had for many years been a servant to Captain Cload's grandfather, said she had often been told how he had seized a Dutch ship, laden with a cargo of cheeses, which had come ashore between Poole Head and North Haven Point. The story goes that he gave some of the sodden cheeses to a Parkstone man

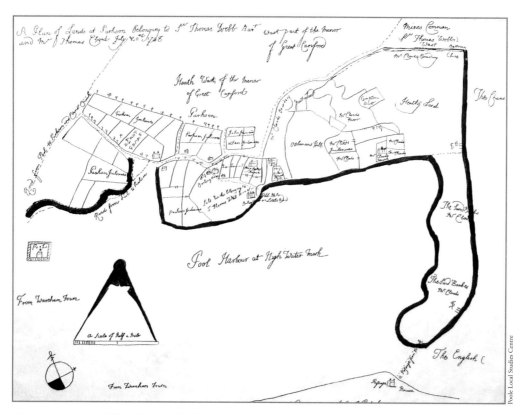

17. A map dated 1748 held in the Poole Local Studies Centre, drawn up to confirm the boundaries between Canford Manor, owned by Sir Thomas Webb Bart., and the Haven Estate owned by Mr Thomas Cload.

called Biddlecombe, who put them in an oven to dry them out, which inevitably *"made them all run into one consistence"*.

Sir Thomas Webb obviously was not successful in his attempt to regain possession of the Haven Estate because, following the court case, a fascinating map was drawn up, presumably on the instructions of the Court, to record their respective ownerships. It is entitled *"A plan of lands at Parkson belonging to Sir Thomas Webb Baronet and Mr Thomas Cload"*. It shows the Haven Estate – annotated as Mr Cload's land – which starts at the top of Evening Hill, extends down to North Haven Point at the tip of Sandbanks, and along the coast to Canford Cliffs Chine and then inland and down today's Lilliput Road. Close to the harbour foreshore is shown "Mr Cload's House", also known as Haven House.

Haven House was without doubt the oldest building in Parkstone-on-Sea. The Poole historian, H.P. Smith, visited it in 1942, noting massive walls of Purbeck stone two feet thick, elements of Tudor brickwork, stone flagged floors and beams of rough-hewn tree trunks. It had been to some extent modernised, and two external elevations given an outer skin of brickwork, but the physical evidence of its antiquity matched the documentary evidence. This latter includes the early 17th century Canford Launnes map which shows a group of four buildings in this location, named as "Haven". The house is then marked consistently

18. Haven House or Flag Farm in a photograph taken about 1875; note the beach on the harbour's edge and the stream flowing down the Luscombe Valley. No other houses are to be seen.

19. The Poole shoreline in the mid 19th century, with its many wooded chines and before any development on the clifftop above, was perfect for landing smuggled goods. Haven House lay a few hundred yards inland from Poole Head in the distance, where the line of the cliffs drops to the sandbanks.

on every map and maritime chart for the next 350 years, although given a variety of names including North Haven House, Lilliput Farm and Flag Farm. It was eventually demolished in the 1990s to make way for modern residential development.

The shores of Poole Bay, with its sandy beaches and secluded wooded chines leading up onto the featureless heath beyond, were ideally suited for the landing of smuggled goods, brought in from France or the Channel Islands by fast lugger. The most notorious and successful of all Dorset's smugglers was Isaac Gulliver, about whom many stories have been told. He certainly landed regular cargoes on these shores, employing such large numbers of local men to carry the tax-free wines, spirits and tea ashore that few of the Revenue men had the resources to tackle him. He died in 1882, aged 77, having achieved respectability in old age and is buried in Wimborne Minster. He left an estate valued at £60,000, a vast sum which would have made him one of the wealthiest men in the county, outside the landed aristocracy.

Haven House was the location of a hastily-convened Coroner's Inquest in March 1765, following the death of a smuggler in a clash with the crew of a Revenue cutter on the north shore of Poole the night before. The Royal Navy cutter 'Folkestone' was on routine patrol, on the lookout for smugglers. A landing party, led by a Lieutenant Down, came across a large gang of smugglers in course of loading contraband goods on to horses for transport inland and, in the ensuing confrontation, Robert Trottman, a smuggler from Kinson, was killed. Trottman's grave can be seen in Kinson churchyard to this day, the headstone declaring that he *"was barbarously murdered on the shore near Poole on 24th March 1765"*. The Coroner from Ringwood had been escorted down to the remote North Haven House the day after the death, where a jury of 'twelve good men and true' consisting of smugglers or their sympathisers swiftly came to a verdict of *"Murder by persons unknown"*. This frustrated any more detailed enquiry by less sympathetic officials in Poole.

The Dorset History Centre holds two detailed maps of the Haven Estate prepared about the time of the Cload's ownership. The earliest of these is undated and entitled 'A Plan of Mr Cload's Estate of Haven'. This makes no attempt to represent the sandbanks accurately, dismissing them as "the Sand Banks, vulgarly called Cales". The lagoon is described as *"Part of Little Sea, now the Salterns"* and, on the north-eastern boundary of the estate, where the track crosses the Luscombe stream, it marks *'The Foord and Passage where the Wains* (wagons can) *pass'*. Obviously, further down the valley the stream was too deep or the land too boggy for wagons to cross. Flaghead Chine is called *"Beacon Chine"*, Canford Cliffs Chine is *"Billman Chine"* beyond which is *"Mines Heath"*. A *"Land Mark Bank"* is shown as separating the estate from the Manor of Great Canford along the line of today's Lilliput Road. Amongst the field names still familiar today is *"Compton Acre"*.

The second map, now referring to the estate as Haven Farm, is believed to have been undertaken about 1770 by the professional mapmaker, Isaac Taylor, who had carried out an extensive survey of Dorset for his comprehensive map of the county published in 1765. It may well have been commissioned for the purposes of the sale of the estate, or perhaps immediately afterwards by the purchaser to establish the extent of his new ownership.

It seems that the Haven Estate was sold off in parts following the death of the last of the Cload descendants in about 1768. A major part, including Haven/Flag Farm, Cload Hill (Lilliput) and the sandbanks were purchased from the executors by Humphrey Sturt of Crichel, near Blandford, who also owned Branksea (Brownsea) Island, which he had acquired in 1765. The Sturt family retained the island and the sandbanks till 1817 when they sold them to Sir Charles Chadd, a substantial landowner of Pinkney Hall at Fakenham in Norfolk, who extended the castle and carried out many improvements before selling

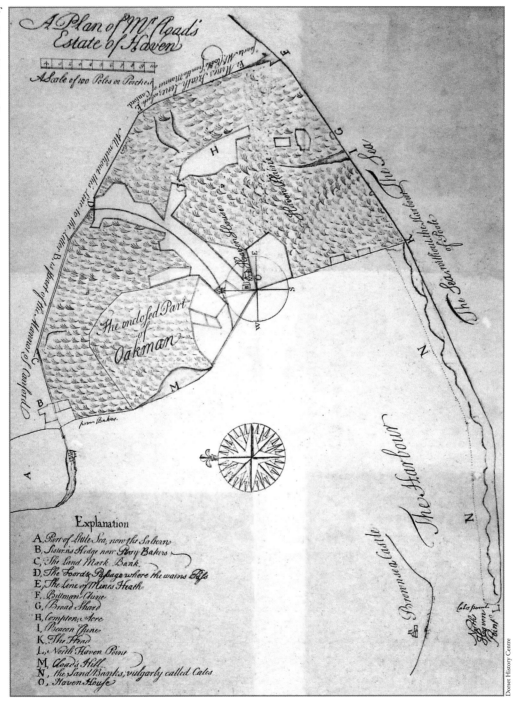

A Plan of Mr Cload's Estate of Haven

A Scale of 100 Poles or Perches

Explanation
A. Part of little Sea, now the Saltern.
B. Sister-ns Hedge near Harry Bakers.
C. The land Mark Bank.
D. The Soord & Passage where the wains Pass
E. The Line of Mines Heath.
F. Billman Chine.
G. Broad Shad.
H. Compton Acre.
I. Beacon Chine.
K. The Head.
L. North Haven Point.
M. Cload's Hill.
N. the Sand Banks, vulgarly called Cates.
O. Haven House.

in 1845 for £14,000. When the sandbanks were re-acquired by the Canford Estate is not clear, but they certainly formed part of Canford Manor again well before the end of the 19th century.

Humphrey Sturt's grandson, Henry, was created the first Baron Alington in 1876, and

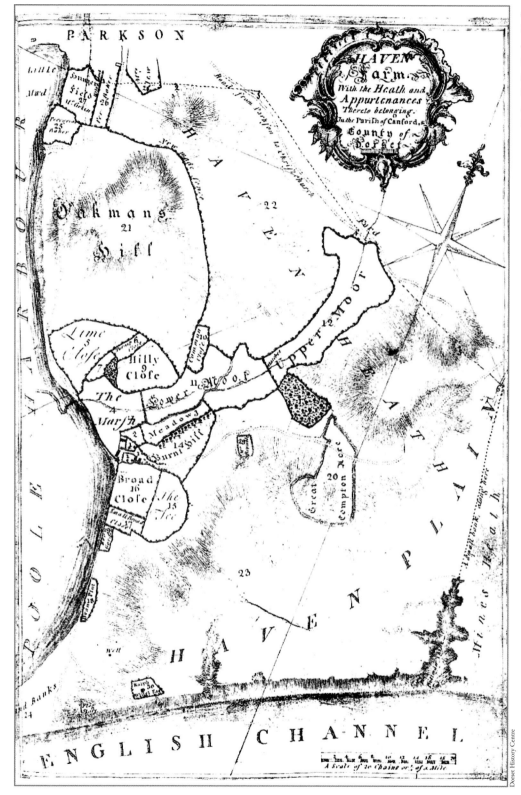

21. Isaac Taylor's map of Haven Farm, believed to have been made in about 1770, from the archives of the Dorset History Centre.

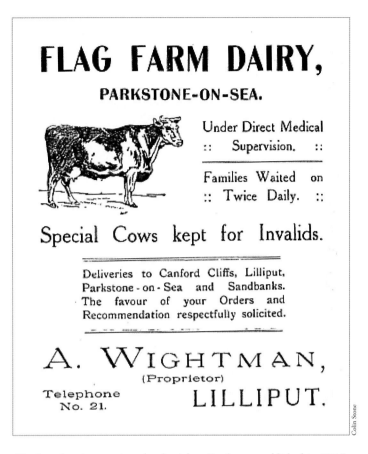

Colin Stone

*22. An advertisement in a local guide to Parkstone published in 1914,
illustrating the dairy services offered by the farmer, Mr Wightman.*

the family continued to own Flag Farm and Lilliput until they sold it in plots for residential development in the 20th century. Whitworth's 1784 chart of Poole Harbour, which first notes the Sturt's ownership, also shows a small plot on Mines Heath (Canford Cliffs) as being the property of Mr Ralph Willets of Merley House, near Wimborne, and in the Tithe map of 1853 he is still listed as owning a house and garden on this clifftop.

The farmer was still advertising his dairy business in a local guide in 1914, but by 1925 the ancient farmhouse had been stripped of most of its land and was sold by Lord Alington to a well-known London architect, J. J. Joass. It survived as a private house until the 1990s, on what, by today's standards, was a spacious plot on the corner of Shore Road and Brudenell Avenue. In 1991 a large extension was added, which may well have altered its character, and in June 1995 Poole Council gave planning permission for it to be demolished and replaced with the three dwellings which are still there today. That this important part of Poole's heritage could be so casually lost defies belief!

The Haven Estate

23. *Flag Farm, previously known as Haven, Haven House and Lilliput Farm, was the oldest house in Parkstone-on-Sea, dating from at least 1600. Located close to the harbour shore at the bottom of Luscombe Valley, it cultivated about 70 acres, and was pulled down about 1996. It is seen here before the First World War.*

24. *The view from outside the farm house, looking north-west across the Luscombe Valley and stream, to some of the early villas built on the Lilliput Estate.*

25. Flag Farm, Witley Lake and Sandbanks seen from Crichel Mount, from an Auction Catalogue in 1912 for the sale of plots on Lord Alington's Lilliput Estate. This included Crichel Mount Road, Minterne Road, Alington Road and Bingham Avenue.

26. Flag Farm after its sale by Lord Alington in 1925. Brudenell Avenue is still a narrow, unmade lane.

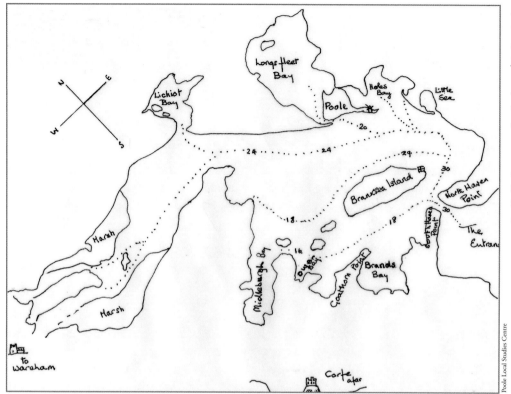

27. Copy of a very early chart of Poole Harbour, prepared about 1662 for Sir Edward Heath who had a plan to recover some 'drowned lands'. This shows the lagoon on the northern shore marked as 'Little Sea'.

Poole Local Studies Centre

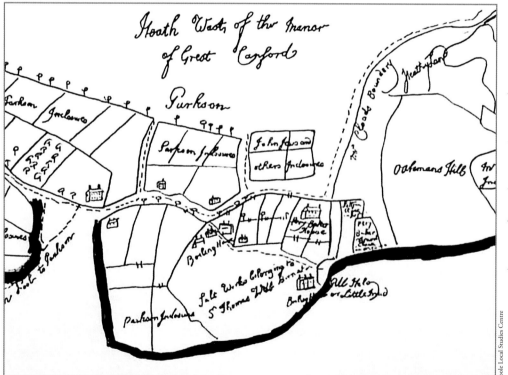

28. Extract from the map prepared in 1748 to show the boundaries between Canford Manor, then held by Sir Thomas Webb Bart., and The Haven Estate owned by Mr Thomas Cload. This clearly describes the area of today's lagoon and adjoining land as "Salt Works" and marks two Boiling Houses.

Poole Local Studies Centre

Chapter 4:

The Salterns

The original objective of all the research which led to this book was to establish the origins and purpose of the muddy tidal backwater at Lilliput that is now known by the very inappropriate name of 'The Blue Lagoon'. In past centuries it has been called 'Gost's Bay', 'Little Sea', the 'salterns' and 'Salterns Marsh'.

Today it carries almost every possible conservation label: it is part of the Poole Harbour Special Protection Area, it is designated as a Site of Special Scientific Interest and is part of a Wetland of International Importance under the RAMSAR Convention. But one thing that has come through loud and clear from this research is that this is definitely not an untouched natural backwater of the harbour. It is, in fact, a derelict war-damaged industrial site, and has been used for industry since at least the early 1700s.

The earliest chart showing the lagoon is in Dorset History Centre, prepared in about 1662 for a Sir Edward Heath, who had a plan to recover some 'drowned lands'. The original chart is now very fragile and almost indecipherable, and has been copied for clarity. Unusually, it was initially drawn upside down, as if the cartographer were standing on the north shore of the harbour, looking south. All the usual features of the harbour are recognisable, although a number of the names have changed – for example: what we now know as Parkstone Bay is marked on this, as it is on all early charts, as Holes Bay; and today's Holes Bay is called as Longsfleet Bay. The lagoon is called *"Little Sea"*.

Some ten years later comes the first written reference to the lagoon, in a lease granted by King Charles II to the Duke of Richmond and Gordon, who was Lord-Lieutenant of the County of Dorsetshire. This was a lease of all the tidal mudlands in the harbour, for 31 years at an annual rent of 5 shillings, on the condition that the Duke constructed an embankment around those mudlands and drained them. Every bay we know today is described clearly in the lease, and the lagoon is listed as *"Gost's Bay, or little sea, bounded almost round by Parkstone"* with an area of 41 acres. This ambitious reclamation scheme never did happen: if it had, the Duke would have gained an estate of some 8,000 acres of reclaimed land, and the harbour would be a very different shape from the one we know today.

The map prepared in 1748 following a legal dispute between Sir Thomas Webb and Mr Thomas Cload did resolve the question as to the original purpose of the lagoon. The whole area of the lagoon, together with what is now Salterns Way and Lilliput shops, is explicitly described as the *"salt works belonging to Sir Thomas Webb baronet"*. Two boiling houses, where the salt was crystallised, are also clearly marked.

Exactly when the lagoon was first used for salt production is difficult to establish.

There have, in fact, been salt-works or salterns in and around Poole Harbour since the Iron Age, and the Domesday Book lists salt-works at Ower, on the southern shore. However only one historical reference suggests that the lagoon could have had such an early use for salt making. In about 1150 there is a reference to a saltern belonging to the Manor of Canford which supplied salt to the Priory of St Michael at Breamore. This saltern was described as being located on Canford's own shores at "*Waldeslete*". Now, whether Waldeslete is the Blue Lagoon, we will probably never know, but there are few other places within the Canford Manor which are likely contenders.

The first specific mention of the Parkstone salterns is in relation to a particularly gruesome murder. In December 1740, the Salisbury Journal reports on the inquest into the death of Joan Mew, a young woman from Witchampton whose pregnant body had been found murdered on a Bye-road on the Heath at "Parkson near Pool" . Her head was nearly severed from her body and by her side was a bloody penknife. A few months later, Henry Smith "*the owner of a saltworks at Parkstone*" was tried at Dorchester Assizes and found guilty of her murder and was sentenced to be hanged in chains at the place where the body was found.

The salterns again appear in court records only a year or so later when the Lord of the Manor, then Sir John Webb, took action to recover possession of "*the salterns at Parkstone*" from his tenant, a Mr Cleeves, who held the land on lease from both Canford Manor and Poole Corporation, each of whom claimed title to it. In his evidence, Mr Cleeves stated that "*the salt-works* [meaning the boiling houses] *were above high water mark and, before they were erected, cattle fed on the land as part of the common of the manor*". So, if Mr Cleeves' could remember the construction of the boiling houses, it is a reasonable deduction that the use of the lagoon for salt production started perhaps some 20 or so years earlier, possibly in the 1720s or 1730s.

So, what was a salt-works like in the 18th century? How did our forefathers extract salt from seawater in England's less-than-sunny climate? Many will be familiar with salt pans in

29. Salt pans in France today. The lagoon at Parkstone would have been sub-divided into rectangular ponds such as these.

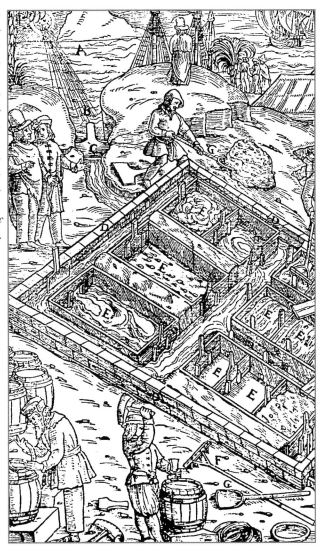

30. A 16th century woodcut illustrating salt making, much as described by Celia Fiennes. At the top of the picture the seawater is channelled into the boiling house, into metal pans beneath which is a turf fire. As the salt crystallises, it is shovelled off into barrels for distribution.

Mediterranean lands: there the seawater is left to stand in rectangular ponds until it is evaporated by the sun to leave salt behind. In our climate, evaporation alone has never been an option, but we do have an excellent contemporary account. Celia Fiennes was one of that breed of redoubtable English lady travellers who kept a journal. In about 1698 she journeyed to Lymington, where she inspected their salterns and described the salt making process:-

"The sea water they draw into trenches by sluces at high tides, and so into several ponds where it stands for the sun to exhale the watry fresh part of it. When they think its fit to boyle they draw off the water from the ponds by pipes which convey it into a house full of large square iron and copper pans; these are shallow and a yard or two square, fixed in rows, may be 20 on a side, in a house under which is a furnace that burns fiercely to keep these pans boiling apace. As the salt candys about the edges or bottom, they shovel it up and fill it in great baskets, and the thinner parts run out into moulds where it forms salt cakes. As fast as they shovel out the boiling salt they refill the pans with sea water from their pipes and keep the furnaces burning night and day."

A very observant lady was Celia Fiennes – the daughter of a General in Cromwell's army. She had earlier visited Brownsea Island, where she gives an equally clear description of the manufacture of copperas. The furnaces which crystallised the salt would have been fired on turf, dug on the heath which then stretched inland from the salterns as far as Christchurch and Ringwood. This was an ideal fuel for salt-making because, not only was it available free from common land, but it also burned slowly and steadily, without the variations of wood. Brine does not have to reach boiling point to crystallise salt, but needs to be kept at a steady temperature.

39   The Salterns

Poole Local Studies Centre

31. Extract from the first Ordnance Survey map, published in 1811. The network of small ponds used to stand seawater at the salterns prior to boiling can clearly be seen in the area o, today's lagoon. The notation "Salterns" refers to the name of the large house which overlooked the saltworks.

Canford Manor's salt works did not last long into the 19th century. They are clearly shown on the first Ordnance Survey map published in 1811, but are no longer marked on a later survey by the Greenwoods in 1825-6. John Sydenham, in his history of Poole published in 1838 says that the salterns *"are now in ruins, not having been worked for many years."*

By 1820, the Napoleonic wars had ended and trade across the Channel had resumed; salt made by boiling over peat fires was not competitive with that made by Continental sunshine. Competition was also growing at home: the repeal of the Salt Tax Acts in 1825 encouraged increased production from the underground deposits of salt in Cheshire at much lower cost. Many English coastal saltworks were closing down, and this was one of them. Nevertheless, it is absolutely clear that commercial salt-making was the principal activity in Parkstone for about 100 years, from the early 1700s to the second decade of the 1800s. Its legacy remains today in the names of Salterns Way and Salterns Marina, and both the censuses and the records of Poole Council confirm that what we today call Sandbanks Road was, until as late as 1900, known as Salterns Road – the road from Poole to the salterns.

Chapter 5

George Jennings
& South Western Pottery

32. The only known portrait of George Jennings.

The one man who, more than any other, changed the face of Parkstone was Josiah George Jennings, the creator of South Western Pottery. This huge industrial-scale factory for the manufacture of sewerage pipes, bricks and ornamental terracotta was, for more than 100 years, the largest employer in the area. Jennings built a pier at the salterns to ship materials, and connected it to the pottery and Parkstone Station with a full-gauge railway line used by his own steam engine and wagons. He built his own farm, and provided cottages for his workers and a school for their children.

Josiah George Jennings was born in the small New Forest village of Eling, near Southampton on 10th November 1810, the eldest of six children of Josiah and Mary Jennings. In his youth he learned his trade working for his uncle who had a large plumbing business at Southwick but, aged 21, he headed for London where he got a job as a plumber with a firm where his father had once been a foreman. In 1836 he married Mary Gill and, in 1838, on the strength of a small inheritance from his grandmother, he set up his own business at Paris Street, Lambeth. Here he had the freedom to experiment with inventions to improve drainage and sanitary ware, which led to a string of ground-breaking patents.

As it entered the Victorian age, London was thriving. Jennings was one of those pioneering inventors and entrepreneurs who characterised the period, and he was to become the leading sanitary engineer of his day. He won the first of many awards for industrial innovation in 1847, when Prince Albert presented him with the Medal of the Society of Arts for his *"indiarubber tube taps for water supply"*. The Prince Consort remained a strong supporter until his untimely death, and Jennings installed the first ever Public Conveniences at the Great Exhibition in 1851. Initially there was reluctance to have anything as indelicate as *"Retiring Rooms"* within the Crystal Palace in Hyde Park, so Jennings offered to carry out the installation at his own expense, provided he could charge one penny to each user. The records show that 827,280 people "spent a penny" to use his flushing closets and, when later the whole building was transported to Sydenham, his facility continued to produce an income of £1,000 a year!

Jennings believed that *"the civilisation of a people can be measured by their domestic and sanitary appliances"*, and he enthusiastically promoted the idea of providing public conveniences that would be accessible in the street. He managed to overcome the objections that such things would give offence to the delicate sensibilities of passers-by by designing them underground, marked by graceful cast-iron superstructures and lit by elegant lamps. Again he offered to install them at no cost to the public, provided that the attendants whom he provided might make a small charge for the use of the closets and a towel. The City of London was eventually persuaded, and the first ever public convenience in this country was opened at the Royal Exchange in 1854. The idea soon spread throughout the land, and by 1895 the firm's catalogue lists 36 towns, as well as 30 railway companies, supplied with Jennings' public toilets.

Jennings' business prospered: he is credited with the installation of the first flushing sanitary facilities in Buckingham Palace, and he undertook the plumbing for the Royal Opera House, rebuilt on the Duke of Bedford's Covent Garden Estate in 1858: to this day, accessible only from what was once the Duke's private box, is a WC containing a magnificent example of a china pan with blue decoration and emblazoned with *"George Jennings Patented, hydraulic and sanitary engineers, Palace Wharf, Lambeth"*. He led the government commission sent out to Sebastopol in 1855 at the request of Florence Nightingale to improve the sanitary conditions at Scutari Hospital, and supplied shower cabinets and baths to the Khedive of Egypt and the Empress Eugenie of France. His designs for water closets, urinals, baths, Turkish baths, saunas, etc, were exported all over the world.

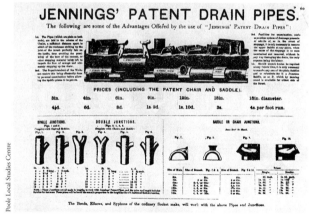

Poole Local Studies Centre

33. A magnificent example of a George Jennings Patented water closet in blue and white china, beneath a mahogany seat, installed in the Duke of Bedford's private box at the Royal Opera House in Covent Garden, and still in use today.

34. A page from South Western Pottery's catalogue for 1874, illustrating Jennings' drainpipe design that was the original reason that he came to Parkstone.

Jennings' achievements seem often to have been confused with the memorably-named Thomas Crapper, also a very talented sanitary engineer, who set up business in London some 15 years later than Jennings. In essence, Crapper was the first to design and patent an effective WWP – a Waste Water Preventer, or overhead cistern to control the amount of water used for each flush of the lavatory. George Jennings had earlier perfected the design of the lavatory pan. We should be grateful to them both.

In 1854, Jennings patented a new design for stoneware sewerage pipes which had an innovative jointing system. This enabled a run of piping to be reopened at a later date, either to clear a blockage or to connect a new branch. Initially, he was unable to find a manufacturer in London interested in making these, so he resolved to set up his own pottery to do so. His search for a site eventually focussed on part of Canford Manor at Parkstone; this not only had a deep seam of suitable clay, but also was sufficiently close to Poole Harbour to enable economical transport of the finished product by ship to his wharf on the Thames at Lambeth, virtually opposite the Palace of Westminster.

Jennings' interest in Parkstone may well have been prompted by an advertisement in the Poole & South Western Herald dated 18th May 1854, offering *"to Potters, Pipemakers and Others"* an existing pottery *"to be let with immediate possession"*. This was a relatively small undertaking known as Blake Hill Pottery in Blake Hill Pottery Road, now called Elgin Road. When this first started operations is not clear: it is not shown on the 1825 Greenwood's map. It was located on land farmed by a local family called Bryant, and in the census of 1851 a member of the household of Francis Bryant was a potter called William Tooth. It was certainly later known as Bryant's Pottery, and was eventually reported in the Poole Herald as having been utterly destroyed by fire on 13th May 1906.

In 1856 George Jennings purchased Seaview Farm, some 70 acres of farmland lying between Parkstone Village and the now-disused salterns, under which lay a seam of clay. The bulk of this land was purchased from local farmers, George Hiley and his son Haviland, with some adjacent areas leased from Canford Manor. Here he built South Western Pottery, which was to be a major influence on the area for more than 100 years. Until it closed in 1966, South-Western Pottery was the largest employer and biggest business in the whole of Parkstone.

Starting with a clean slate, Jennings had the opportunity to develop a pottery

35. South Western Pottery in 1870.

Poole Local Studies Centre

incorporating the very latest ideas in the field, and the result must have astonished the nearby residents of Parkstone Village. A massive range of three and four-storey red brick factory buildings, punctuated by seven towering chimneys, rose from the virgin farmland. These, together with more than a dozen round kilns, drying sheds, engine and pump houses, and stabling for the horses, were all located almost in the middle of his 70 acre site, reached by Pottery Road. To manage the enterprise he recruited John Hudson, the manager of the Bourne Valley Pottery which had started production at Branksome few years earlier.

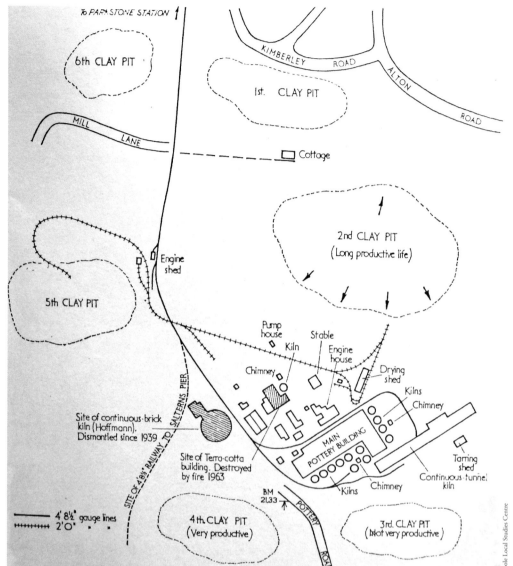

36. A sketch plan of South Western Pottery showing the locations of the clay workings.

The first clay pit to be dug was to the north of the site, close to where Kimberley Road now runs, and is today occupied by a block of flats called Lilliput Court. This pit was linked to the main complex, as were all six of the pits eventually excavated on the site, by a light horse-drawn tramway to transport the clay from its source to the pottery.

For the first half century, the clay was cut by gangs of men using long spades, and it wasn't till early in the 20th Century that steam-driven excavating machines came into use.

Parkstone's clay was not suitable for fine tableware and ornaments like those, for example, produced later on by Poole Pottery, nor was this what Jennings intended. He needed a clay which would make tough heavy-duty pipes, bricks and terracotta ornamental-facing-blocks to meet the demands of the 19th century building boom. South Western Pottery soon became a huge industrial-scale manufacturer of a wide range of these goods

and a number of its catalogues for the period survive, illustrating the various products.

The pottery provided work for many in the district, and an examination of the census returns shows how the predominantly agricultural employment opportunities in the area in the 1840s -1850s changed markedly after the pottery opened. In 1861 the pottery employed

39. Jennings' pier at the salterns, completed in 1867. This was not finally demolished until the construction of Salterns Marina in 1973.

115 men and boys, a significant proportion of the entire population of Parkstone shown in the census at 1,134 people. However, the pottery was not welcomed with universal enthusiasm across Parkstone-on-Sea, and letters in the local press complained bitterly about the smoke and dust it generated.

40. The third of South Western Pottery's steam engines, the "George Jennings", standing outside the pottery buildings in the 1950s.

The pottery's kilns required large quantities of coal, which at first was brought in by Jennings own ships from Newcastle-on-Tyne to Poole Quay, whence they shipped out the finished pipes to his wharf on the Thames at Lambeth. Jennings and the Harbour Board were always arguing about the harbour dues. In

41. The 'George Jennings' steam engine emerging from the private line from South Western Pottery, into the shunting yard at Parkstone Station.

addition, it was slow and inefficient to transport such bulky materials by horse and cart over almost three miles of unmade roads from Poole Quay. So in 1866, Jennings applied to the Board of Trade for permission to build a pier at the salterns, which were much closer to the pottery, contending that this would free him from the obligation to pay Harbour Dues. This was hotly contested by the Quay Committee of Poole Corporation, but it had to admit that such a pier would not cause an obstruction to shipping the harbour, so permission was granted.

This pier was completed in 1867, and Jennings wrote to his son *"Instead of ships taking our coal to Poole Quay, they deliver it at once to my coal store at the salterns, and I ship off my pipes from the same place"*. With much reluctance due to the high legal costs involved, the Corporation took Jennings to court over non-payment of Harbour Dues. The case was not settled until late in 1873, when the Court of Common Pleas found in favour of the Corporation, ordering Jennings to pay its costs of £2,789 in addition to his own. Nevertheless, the pier had been built and South Western Pottery continued to use it until after the First World War.

At first Jennings linked the pier to the pottery with a light horse-drawn tramway, similar to those that were already in use within the clay beds themselves. However in 1872, the year the railway eventually came to Poole, he made a substantial investment by purchasing a brand new full-gauge saddle-tank steam engine, and negotiated with Canford Manor to lease the additional land to lay railway-lines northward to connect with the main line at Parkstone Station, which was to open two years later, in 1874.

Soon permanent rail lines were also laid to Salterns Pier for hauling the coal and pipes. Exactly when these were constructed is not clear, because surprisingly the lines are not shown on any of the Ordnance Survey maps until 1924, just before they finally ceased to be used, but most authorities agree that they must have been laid very soon after 1874. A court case reported in August 1928 confirms that the line to the pier was still there at that date, but it had been removed by the early thirties. However, that from the Pottery up to Parkstone Station remained in place until the pottery closed in the 1960s, and many are the tales of schoolboys cadging rides on the little green engine as it puffed its way up the hill to the main line junction.

There were, in fact, three steam engines used at the Pottery between 1872 and 1966. The first was an 0-4-0 saddle-tank engine built by Fox Walker of Bristol in 1872. This was replaced in 1893 by an 0-6-0 inside-cylinder saddle-tank engine, by Peckett of Bristol, which was heavier and with a longer wheelbase. It was the first to be called the "George Jennings" after the pottery's proprietor, who had been tragically killed 10 years earlier. This second engine may have been too heavy for the line, because it was replaced in 1902 with another 0-4-0 saddle-tank engine by Peckett, also called the "George Jennings", which was still in use when the pottery eventually closed, more than 60 years later. Most photographs are of this engine, as is that on the adjacent page.

Jennings had an enlightened attitude towards his employees, who by all accounts regarded him with some affection. He built a terrace of cottages for them, still to be seen in Pottery Road, and a school for their children opposite the Beehive Inn, close to his pier and coal-yard, by the old salterns. His pride and joy was his "Model Farm", close to the Sandbanks Road at Whitecliff. Only part of his 70 acres was being used for clay production at any one time; the rest was still good grazing land. So, in about 1875, using his own bricks and other materials from his pottery, Jennings built an idealised set of farm buildings,

42. *The line of Jennings' railway ran from Salterns Pier, along what is today Lagoon Road, crossed the Sandbanks Road near the Lilliput Sailing Club, across open fields, crossing Elgin Road, skirting round the Cemetery, past the Model Farm and so up to the pottery itself. From there it continued northward into the shunting yard at Parkstone main-line station. This is shown on an extract from the 1924 Ordnance Survey.*

43. The Model Farm and Edenhurst, pictured soon after they were built by George Jennings in about 1875. The photographer is standing on today's Whitecliff playing fields, and the Sandbanks Road crosses the centre of the picture.

Andrew Hawkes' Poole Picture Archive

including a house for his Bailiff who managed the farm, on which were also employed 8 men and 3 boys. Next to the farm he had also built a fine villa called 'Edenhurst' in which his daughter, Miss Cathy Jennings, lived in later life, although earlier censuses show the Pottery Manager living in it.

Although George Jennings initially came to Parkstone because of its clay, he became very attached to the area, and bought a small estate at Castle Eve, at the top of Sandecotes Road. Here he would spend holidays with his large family; his first wife, Mary, with whom he had four children had died in 1844, but he remarried five years later to Sophia Budd, and they had another eleven children. They were staying at Castle Eve Villa at the time of the census in 1871, where George is entered as the head of the household, aged 60, and described as "*Brick & pottery manufacturer employing 150 men and 20 boys; Farmer of 70 acres employing 8 men and 3 boys; and Shipowner employing 20 men*". With him were his second wife, Sophia, aged 39, and children Catherine 31, Percy 8, Ethel 5, Florence 4 and Bertie 1, together with a cook, housemaid and nurse.

George Jennings died unexpectedly in 1882, in a traffic accident on Albert Bridge, when being driven back to his home in Nightingale Lane, Clapham by one of his sons. The horse pulling their gig shied, and threw him against a dustcart. He was 72. However, his sons continued to run South Western Pottery until 1903, when it was sold to Messrs Thomas Wragg and Sons Ltd., a substantial company from Swadlincote in Derbyshire which specialised in the manufacture of firebricks for the iron and steel industries of Yorkshire. That company invested heavily in modernising the Parkstone works and continued production there for another 50 years. Eventually in 1966 production was closed down and the site was redeveloped for housing as the Conifer Park Estate.

44. Although the exact location of this early 20th century photograph cannot be precisely identified, it is entitled 'A lane towards Sandbanks' and was published as a postcard. It gives an impression of how rural the area was at that time.

45. A pair of 'Lady Wimborne Cottages', built by the Canford Estate in 1873, which can still be seen in Sandbanks Road, although the barn is no longer there.

Chapter 6

Chapter 6

The 19th Century
Buildings & Estates

Exploring Parkstone today, it is clear that it is very densely developed; every possible space contains a house or block of flats, and many older houses with generous gardens are being pulled down to put two in their place. So it takes quite a lot of imagination to visualise the area just over a century ago when, apart from South Western Pottery and the salterns, the rest of Parkstone-on-Sea was a peaceful rural backwater. Narrow unmade country lanes led to open fields and woodlands with a scattering of houses and farms. Most of the buildings which existed at that time vanished long ago, but we do have a record of what some of them were like. It is also clear that a number of far-sighted landowners were optimistic about the future of the area and had started high-class residential development schemes on estates at Lilliput, Canford Cliffs, Branksome Park and at the top of Castle Hill at Castle Eve and Sandecotes.

The oldest building in the area was certainly Haven House, later known as Flag Farm, which faced the harbour at the bottom of the Luscombe Valley. The history of this is covered in some detail in Chapter Three. The early buildings on Sandbanks, in Canford Cliffs, around South Western Pottery and in Parkstone Village are covered in their respective chapters.

Within the rest of Parkstone-on-Sea, there were a number of small farms, but there is only one of those early farm houses still existing: Canford Cottage in Pottery Road, which was occupied in the 1840s and 1850s by George Wareham, a tenant of the Manor, who farmed 22 acres. Although today the house looks from the outside to be built of brick and slate, actually it has cob walls and once had a thatched roof. Inside it is rich in oak beams, inglenook fireplaces and uneven floors. Further down the Sandbanks Road, a pair of 'Lady Wimborne cottages' can still be seen, built by the Manor in 1873.

In addition to the farms and their cottages, there were also just a few rather grander houses which tried to remain aloof from all the other activity. None of these was so large as remotely to resemble a 'stately home'; indeed they were all relatively modest. However they were all surrounded by their own land and occupied by persons of independent means who aspired to gentility. There were also an ancient mill, two yacht clubs which were founded towards the end of the century and a single shop.

Salterns House:

The oldest house still surviving in Parkstone-on-Sea is 'Salterns House', also known as 'The Salterns', which is marked on the 1748 Webb map as *"Perry Baker's house"*. It was originally a small square two-storey house in an early Georgian style, but has been much extended and altered over the centuries. It is still there today, divided into two spacious homes, just off Anthony's Avenue. Internally the handsome timber panelling and ornately carved door and fireplace surrounds give an idea of its original elegance. Salterns stood in its own grounds of some 30 acres stretching down to the Sandbanks and Lilliput Roads, and was approached by a long drive, now Brownsea View Avenue, with a gatehouse. From

46. *"Salterns House" today, now approached from Anthony's Avenue in Lilliput. It is currently divided into two dwellings, and has obviously been much extended on the original small square 18th century house at its centre.*

47. *Captain Frederick Butts of Salterns House.*

its terrace, there were uninterrupted views across fields and marshes to the harbour, which is difficult to credit today, but if the reader refers to Illustration 156 in Chapter 10, it can be clearly seen in about 1918 with an open aspect across the harbour.

Salterns House was purchased by Captain Frederick Butts in 1863 on retiring from the army after Crimea. His grandfather had been a friend and patron of the artist, William Blake, who had bequeathed the family a significant part of his portfolio, and a large Victorian extension was added to the house in which to hang these pictures. Captain Butts was already married when he came to Salterns and had one son, Aubrey, who tragically died aged 22 of pneumonia, caught after a night clinging to the hull of his yacht, wrecked by a squall on Hook Sands.

48. Mary Butts, from dust-jacket of her reminiscences of her childhood, growing up in Salterns House around 1900. It gives a vivid pen-portrait of the area and people of that time.

The Captain took his wife Eleanor sailing in the Mediterranean in an attempt to forget the tragedy and, to compound his grief, whilst visiting a bazaar in Constantinople, she collapsed and died. She was buried in Turkey, and he returned to Salterns a widower.

Some years later Captain Butts married again to a local girl, thirty years his junior, Mary Jane Briggs of Milnthorpe, Alton Road, and they had two children, Mary and Anthony (after whom Anthony's Avenue is named). The daughter Mary, born in 1891, was an accomplished author of the 1930s, with ten books to her credit. One of these was a fascinating autobiography of her

49. The Chapel of the Holy Angels in Lilliput Road, built in 1874 on land given by Captain Butts of Salterns House.

The Chapel of the Holy Angels, Lilliput.

early years called '*The Crystal Cabinet; my childhood at Salterns*' which gives a detailed pen-portrait of the surrounding area about 1900, and the few people who lived there.

The 1891 census shows Job Pike, Capt. Butts' coachman and groom, living in the lodge to Salterns House. His grand-daughter, who was born in that lodge, recalled that, when Capt Butts and his wife wished to go hunting, her grandfather would take their horses to Parkstone station, load them onto the train and accompany them on the journey to Maiden Newton. There they would be stabled overnight and the Butts would follow the next day to hunt with the Blackmore Vale, before returning the same way. Captain Butts gave the land in Lilliput Road on which the Chapel of the Holy Angels was built in 1874, as a chapel-of-ease attached to St Peters at Ashley Cross. He died in 1905 and, after two years, his widow married Major Colville-Hyde of Wilderton, Branksome Park, who had been a regular visitor to Salterns over many years. As Mrs Colville-Hyde, she became a formidable leading figure in Parkstone's Edwardian social circle.

The Elms:

Another large house was The Elms, on the Sandbanks Road. The land on which it stood forms a peninsular of almost 50 acres, today occupied by Elms and Pearce Avenues. This must originally have been part of Canford Manor, but the earliest record of a change of ownership is in July 1809 when it was part of a trust settled on Miss Clara Pointer, prior to her marriage with Mr. Samuel Weston. At this time the maps show that the land was largely fields with a small farm with outbuildings, and a brick-kiln sited on the western shore. However, by 1839 there is reference in a mortgage document to a "*mansion house, lands and hereditaments*", which had replaced the farm house, probably about 1830. The Westons are recorded in the census of 1841 as living there, but by 1851 it is occupied by a farmer, John Tuck, and his widow is still there in 1861, after which the deeds refer to a number of subsequent tenants. In any event, the Westons owned this small estate for 50 years and then put it up for sale by public auction in 1859.

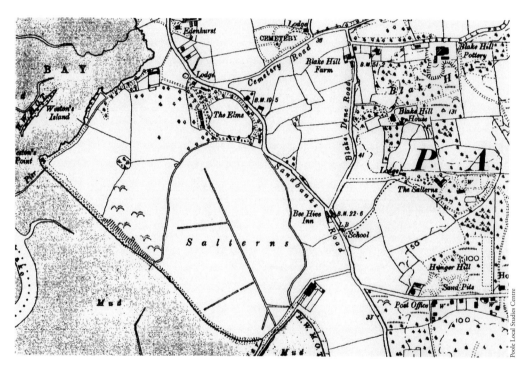

50. This extract from the 1890 Ordnance Survey map shows The Elms, together with a number of the early buildings in the vicinity of the salterns, including Salterns House, Blake Hill Farm and Blake Hill House, Blake Hill Pottery, Edenhurst, and the Bee Hive Inn.

The highest bidder at the auction was a successful local businessman, William Pearce [he after whom Pearce Avenue is named]. He had an iron-foundry on West Quay Road in Poole making agricultural machinery, and eventually became the principal owner of Poole Waterworks. He paid the substantial sum of £3,380 for "*all that mansion house called 'The Elms' with the barns, stables, coach house, backsides [sic] and orchards, walled-in garden and lodge*", together with "*arable meadow or pasture of 45a 1r 15p, and the brick kiln and shed*".

William Pearce was the second owner who did not live at The Elms himself. Buy-to-let is not a new idea! Both at the time of his purchase, and at his death, he is described as living at Springfield House, a very grand house on the hill above Ashley Cross. He died in 1889 and left the estate to his great-nephew, Capt Daniel Pearce Sunderland, who continued to let it to a variety of occupiers including the Rev. Lionel Dawson-Damer, Canon of Salisbury Cathedral who was very prominent in local social circles, probably because his older brother was the 4th Earl Portarlington. The Rev. Lionel died at the Elms, aged only 55, in July 1888, but his widow, Edith, continued to live there till her own death in 1905 – described by the five year old Mary Butts as "*a vast old lady with a red face, in black satin all sewn with shiny beads*".

Captain Sunderland still owned The Elms Estate at the time of its development in the late 1920s. In 1922, a local surveyor and estate agent, Norman Hibbs, successfully applied on Sunderland's behalf for the permission of Poole Council to lay sewers and to construct Elms and Pearce Avenues, although this work does not actually seem to have been carried out until 1926. The intention was to divide the bulk of the 50 acre estate into individual building plots, leaving the main house with a very much reduced garden of 2.5

51. The Elms Estate from a postcard sent in 1939. Development is well under way, but there remain a few plots where houses would be completed after the war.

acres stretching from the main entrance on Sandbanks Road with its gatehouse and separate cottage, to Elms Avenue, including a triangular area of undeveloped backland in the centre of the estate, now known as the Recreation Ground.

Sunderland sold The Elms house in 1925 to Ernest Hawker, a prominent member of Parkstone Yacht Club and owner of the Motor Mac garage business in Holdenhurst Road, Bournemouth, and over the next few years sold off the building plots on the remainder of the estate. These were purchased either individually by owner-occupiers who had houses built to their own design, or in small blocks by speculative builders who put up houses for sale. By the time the war came in 1939, perhaps two-thirds of the houses had been built, and the remainder were completed by the early 1960s.

Ken Latham

52. Elms Lodge on the Sandbanks Road in the 1950s, after it had been sold off separately from the main house. It was sited close to today's entrance to Elms Close.

E.G. Hawker died at The Elms in 1952 and his executors sold off separately the Cottage and the Gatehouse on the Sandbanks Road to help pay Death Duties. However, his widow continued to live in the house until 1963, by which time the building was in a sadly neglected state. On her death the house and remaining garden was purchased at auction by a private property company, which then repurchased the Gatehouse and Cottage and in

Peter Dobson

53. The Elms, a mansion built in the 1830s which originally had a small estate of 50 acres including farm buildings, a brick kiln, staff cottages and a gatehouse onto Sandbanks Road. It is shown in the 1960s following an extensive renovation, but it was soon to be demolished and redeveloped.

1966 obtained planning consent to develop nine houses in Elms Close on that half of its site fronting Sandbanks Road. These houses were built and sold off over the next four years.

The old house was restored to its former glory and was then purchased out of the company by one of the Directors. However, after only a few years, it is said to have succumbed to rampant dry rot, and the owner pulled it down (without, it seems, any protest by Poole Council – yet more of the Borough's heritage lost without a fight) and constructed an undistinguished chalet-style house in its place. A subsequent owner gained permission in 1974 to carve another two building plots out of the Elms Avenue frontage, and at the time of writing, planning consent has been given for the replacement of the Chalet with two 21st century houses. The only trace of the original fields and gardens of the Elms Estate is the open recreation ground which lies largely unseen in the very centre of the estate, and is now owned by the Residents Association.

Parkstone Yacht Club:

What is now Parkstone Yacht Club, originally The Parkstone Boating and Pier Club, was founded on the edge of the Elms Estate in 1895 by a small but enthusiastic band of sailors who moored their boats in Parkstone Bay. At that time Rat Island, a low-lying, grass-covered mud bank, extended almost entirely across the mouth of the bay, protecting the yacht moorings, but it has now been entirely eroded.

Within a year the club members had constructed a short pier and slipway, had raised a loan from the bank and started construction of a clubhouse on concrete stilts at the very edge of Westons Point. The freehold of the land on which it stood was purchased from Lord Wimborne for £30, and an agreement was reached both with him and the Trustees of the Elms Estate to permit access over the lane now known as Turks Lane.

The club's name was soon changed to that of Parkstone Sailing Club and the first yard-hand taken on. It continued to thrive, and survived the First World War with very

54. The first clubhouse and pier of Parkstone Sailing Club at Weston's Point, adjacent to The Elms Estate, photographed in about 1907.

little disruption, so it was a shock in 1918 when it became known that proposals had been approved by Poole Council and the Harbour Commissioners to build a massive shipbuilding yard at Salterns (see Chapter 10). The Committee commissioned a professional valuation of the Club premises, assessed at £1,200. Fortunately the shipyard plans never materialised and the club continued to go from strength to strength.

Parkstone Mill:

The earliest reference to the mill comes in the Last Will and Testament of Thomas Dunford of Longfleet, made in February 1727. In it he leaves to his son Isreal *"my mill at Parkson with all the houses barns stables with all out houses"*. It is marked on Isaac Taylor's map some years later in 1765 and was, of course, part of Canford Manor which, in 1804, leased the *"water grist mill"* to a local merchant, Robert Slade, for a term of 99 years at a rent of £8-13-6d each half year. It is described in the 1811 Ordnance Survey as an "iron mill" and by 1814, Slade is advertising it for sale in the Salisbury and Winchester Journal, described as *"All that Dwelling-house with the adjoining Water Corn Mill and Edge Tool Mill, extensive garden and about eight acres of Ground; most advantageously situated for business at Parkestone, in the county of Dorset, within a short distance of Poole harbour".*

In 1844 the mill is described in the Tithe records as a *"mill and millpond"* but by 1851, although the census refers to a *"mill and mill cottages"*, these are no longer occupied by a miller, but by James Green, a Coastguard, and his wife and six children. No mention of it can be found any later than this, and it seems likely that it vanished beneath South Western Pottery in the late 1850s. The only legacy today is in the name 'Mill Lane' and in the spring which once fed the millpond and now feeds the small ponds off Conifer Avenue.

Blake Dene House:

Not far from The Elms, off Elgin Road, was Blake Dene House, built by Edward Harrison Solly in 1884, having first moved into the adjoining Myrtle Cottage with his wife, Lucy, in 1882 whilst the big house was being completed. Edward and his uncle, Samuel Solly from Swinderby in Lincolnshire, were, like many Parkstone residents, successful businessmen from the north of England who bought extensive areas of land in the area. Edward was the owner of a silk spinning mill in Congleton, Cheshire, employing up to 250 workers, and by 1891 had moved out to Wimborne where he was made a County Magistrate for Wimborne Petty Sessions Division.

Blake Dene House was adjacent to the land of South Western Pottery and was purchased from Solly by the pottery for the occupation of one of George Jennings' sons, Sidney, who had continued to manage the business after his father's death. After the pottery was sold in 1903 to Thomas Wragg and Sons Ltd, the house was occupied by Mr Horace Wragg. Then, immediately following the Second World War, the house had a brief spell as the Dorset Country Club.

Next to Blake Dene House was a small farm, known originally as Myrtle Farm, then Blake Dene Farm and latterly Pottery Farm. The farmhouse dated from the 17th century, built of cob with a thatched roof, and was demolished in the 1950s. Its land and the main house were redeveloped with the rest of the Pottery Estate in the early 1960s, forming part of Crawshaw Road, named after the last Manager of South Western Pottery whose home it was before and during the war.

55. Blake Dene House, in what was then Blake Dene Pottery Road (now Elgin Road) built by Edward Solly JP in 1884. It became the Dorset Country Club for a few years after the Second World War, before being demolished as part of the Conifer Park development.

56. Pottery Farm at Blake Hill, just before it was demolished in the 1950s. It now forms part of the Conifer Park development.

Andrew Hawkes' Poole Picture Archive

The 19th Century Building & Estates

Blake Hill House:

The maps published in the mid 1800s show a 'Blake Hill Farm' on the east side of Blake Dene Road, occupied in 1851 by Francis Bryant, 'land proprietor', but by 1902 this building seems to have been enlarged and renamed 'Blake Hill House'. No photograph has been found, but planning applications were made in the late 1950s to redevelop the extensive grounds with what is now Partridge Drive, Partridge Walk and the upper part of Brownsea View Avenue.

57. Blake Hill Farm and cottages in Blake Dene Road, taken about 1910, looking west towards the junction with Elgin Road. South Western Pottery lies behind the trees in the distance.

58. A slightly later picture of Blake Hill Farm, looking from the opposite direction down Blake Dene Road towards Salterns; by this time it was known as Viney's Farm.

59. Blake Hill Cottages were very typical of Victorian farm workers cottages. These were built of local bricks, possibly from South Western Pottery.

Blake Hill Farm:

This farmhouse was located on the west side of Blake Dene Road, close to its junction with Elgin Road (previously known as 'Blake Hill Pottery Road'). The buildings have been shown in this position since about 1800, but were not described by the name 'Blake Hill Farm' until the publication of the 1902 Ordnance Survey: the same time that the neighbouring Blake Hill Farm was aggrandised into 'Blake Hill House'. Perhaps there is a connection.

The farm had been owned since at least the 1840s by the Bryant family, who farmed all the fields between Blake Hill and the salterns. Also on their land was the small Blake Hill Pottery (see Chapter 5) which had been worked even before South Western Pottery was developed, but burned down in 1906. By 1890, the farm had been bought by Charles Viney who came from Fordingbridge with his wife Ann. He died in 1899 but, with their five sons, his widow continued farming until the 1930s. No trace of the farm remains today; its fields are completely covered by the bungalows of Austin Avenue and Blake Dene Road. However, the family must have retained some land because, within living memory, they continued to sell market garden produce in a popular shop in Ashley Cross.

Heathside:

Another of the original houses of the gentry was 'Heathside', built about 1840 in the style of an Italianate two-storey villa, including a separate gatehouse on the Sandbanks

60. This is believed to be 'Heathside' at 355 Sandbanks Road, photographed early in the 20th Century. Built about 1840, it was pulled down and redeveloped as the 'Avalon' housing estate in the 1970s.

Road. It may well have been built by Samuel Solly who is shown in occupation in the 1841 census, and enjoyed extensive grounds close to the top of Evening Hill. Before all the trees grew up, it would have had wide-ranging views over the harbour and is recalled with affection by Mary Butts of Salterns House as a *"small, low house, set in a wood, with a wild garden"*. It had a set of ilex trees *"enormous and of great age....that grew on rough lawn in front of the house, turf so rough that it was purple with orchids in spring"*.

Samuel Solly died in 1847 and his widow, Dorothea, moved to Myrtle Cottage at Blake Dene.

Heathside was pulled down in about 1972 but redevelopment of the extensive site of almost 8 acres did not commence until 1977. It now consists of 24 houses and two blocks of flats, today known as 'Avalon'.

61. Lilliput House in Alington Road on Evening Hill, built by Lord Alington in 1889 as a summer home for his family, when they were not staying at Crichel House near Wimborne or their London home in Portman Square. From a postcard sent in 1907.

Lilliput House:

There has been a 'Lilliput House' on the prominent site halfway up Evening Hill, on the corner of Alington Road, since at least the 1780s, but by 1825 this was described on the Greenwoods' map as 'ruins'. However, this seems to be the first recorded use of the name 'Lilliput'.

A second Lilliput House was rebuilt on the 12 acre site in 1889 by Henry Gerard Sturt, 1st Baron Alington. Although the family's ancestral seat was at Crichel, north-east of Blandford, and there was a large London house in Portman Square, he wanted a summer home for his family on the land he owned overlooking Poole Harbour. This new house was vast, designed in the mock-Tudor style by architect John Birch with 14 bedrooms, two bathrooms, drawing room, dining room, winter garden, music room, billiard room and extensive domestic offices and staff accommodation. Outside was a Gatehouse at the bottom of the main entrance drive, and a second drive leading to a substantial stable block

with accommodation for four carriages and eight horses, which would later house Lord Alington's Rolls Royce.

Lord Alington's interest in the house may not have lasted long because, by the 1901 census, it is shown as occupied by the Rev. Henry Watkins, his wife Marie and their 20 year-old son Henry G. It took 15 staff, domestics, gardeners and coachmen to look after them!

The main house is one of the few original houses on the Lilliput Estate which still exists, although part of it has been demolished and the remainder converted into two spacious dwellings. The stable block, known as 'Little Court', has also been converted to two dwellings which are now separately owned.

The Lilliput Estate:

The Sturt family, later to become the Barons Alington, owned the Manor of More Crichel, a vast agricultural estate between Wimborne and Blandford. In about 1768, Charles Sturt had purchased a large part of the Haven Estate from the executors of Thomas Cload, including the Luscombe Valley, the 80 acre Flag Farm and Lilliput, (which we know today as Evening Hill, after the name of one of the early villas, on the site which is now occupied by the Lewis-Manning Hospice). A century later, in the late 1870s, a descendant, now 'Lord' Alington, instructed his Estate Manager to set out a series of roadways on the land at Lilliput which were to become Crichel Mount, Alington and Minterne Roads, Mount Grace Drive and Bingham Avenue. He then offered ground leases on generously-sized building plots for the construction of substantial villas, many of which enjoyed spectacular views over the harbour and Purbeck Hills.

The first of these villas was 'Luscombe' where the lease commenced in December 1880, immediately next to the site of Lilliput House. It was soon to be followed by Witley, Evening Hill, Minterne Grange, Mount Grace, Landfall, Whinthorpe and Grayrigg. By 1900 there was a select group of large 'gentleman's residences' established on the Lilliput

63. Three of the early 'gentleman's residences' built on Lord Alington's Lilliput Estate. From right to left are Luscombe, Witley and Evening Hill.

64. This picture of Bingham Avenue was taken soon after 1900 on the Lilliput Estate. The estate roads were initially single-track with a gravelled surface, but the new houses were very substantial.

Andrew Hawkes' Poole Picture Archive

Estate, which were in marked contrast to the more modest dwellings elsewhere in the district. Today, most of these original villas have been replaced with one, or more often several, modern houses or blocks of flats. However, one large Victorian pile, Grayrigg, remains as a single family house today, although occupying only a fraction of its original site of more than seven acres. It originally had stables, a squash court, tennis court and beautifully landscaped gardens with terraces and lily ponds. From 1908 it was the home of Harold Soames, whose daughter Olave married Sir Robert Baden-Powell of Scouting fame at St Peters Church, Lower Parkstone, in 1912.

65. This photograph of Lilliput Road comes from a postcard sent in 1913, but the photo could have been taken at any time after the turn of the century. It shows the Rogers' general store and some of the cottages built for local workmen and staff at the big houses on Lord Alington's Lilliput Estate.

Andrew Hawkes' Poole Picture Archive

66. The Post Office and general store at 22 Lilliput Road. It was opened in 1897 by George Rogers, seen here with his wife Mary and four children. The family continued to run the shop until 1965.

In September 1912, the "Second Portion of the Flag Farm & Lilliput Building Estate" was offered by auction at the Canford Cliffs Hotel by a London firm of Auctioneers on behalf of Lord Alington. This comprised rather smaller plots situated at the northern end of Bingham Avenue and on the other side of Luscombe Valley in Brudenell Avenue, Brudenell Road, Nairn Road and Canford Crescent.

On the northern side of the Lilliput Estate, fronting Lilliput Road, lay what Mary Butts described as *"the slum-village of Lilliput"*, with a number of impoverished dwellings occupied by labourers and their families. Gradually these were replaced with more substantial, but still modest brick cottages, built particularly for those working in the big houses. Many of these are still there today. This was still a distinct community from that at Salterns, and was centred around the Chapel of the Holy Angels, the Mission Hall and the shop and Post Office. Although there was no pub, the single-storey 'Lilliput Working Men's Village Club', the gift of Mr Francis Beckford of Witley in Crichel Mount Road, acted as the social centre.

The Post Office and general store at No.22 Lilliput Road was opened in 1897 and, at the time, was the only shop in Parkstone-on-Sea outside Parkstone Village. It was run by George Rogers who had recently come out of the Royal Navy, and his wife Mary and they, and their descendants, continued the business until 1965, when they sold to Leslie and Dolly Dale. The building remains today virtually unaltered, and will be remembered by many as 'Mr Dale's shop'. A little further up Lilliput Road at the turn of the century was a bakehouse.

East Dorset Sailing Club:

At the foot of Evening Hill today stands what is probably the oldest yacht club in the harbour, the East Dorset Sailing Club. Like Parkstone Yacht Club, it was originally founded by a group of sailors who kept their boats on moorings reached from the same pier, and has formal records going back to 1896 as the 'Whitley Lake Pier Committee'. However there is strong evidence that it began much further back, probably in about 1875. An early member was Francis Beckford, a wealthy "West India merchant", who in 1890 built the house named 'Witley', overlooking the pier and was the donor of the Lilliput Working Men's' Village Club in Lilliput Road.

The sailing club still uses the same pier, much repaired and renewed over more than a century, but the old corrugated iron hut remembered by some older members has been replaced by a more practical, but sadly no more beautiful, two-storey brick clubhouse, built about 1969.

67. Whitley Pier, built or substantially extended in 1892 by the forerunner of the East Dorset Sailing Club. On the right of the picture is one of the harbour's leading lights for shipping and a house called Whinthorpe on Lord Alington's Lilliput Estate.

68. A second picture of Whitley Pier, showing the slipway which originally allowed small boats to be launched and recovered. The shape of the harbour wall has subsequently changed at this point.

Andrew Hawkes' Poole Picture Archive

69. A rare (and much repaired) photograph taken in 1880 showing Lord Sidney Osborne's house, The Hive, on today's Shore Road at the bottom of Chaddesley Glen. The road, however, does not yet exist and access to the sandbanks is along the foreshore. Parts of the sea wall can still be seen today in front of Hive Gardens, the bungalow estate built on the site.

Poole Local Studies Centre

The Hive:

Another of the very early houses was The Hive, on the harbour shore at the bottom of Haven Hill. This is noted in the census for 1851 as being under construction, but ten years later is shown as completed, occupied by a gardener and domestic servant. This was a very substantial summer holiday home, built by the memorably-named Reverend Lord Sidney Godolphin Osborne, the younger brother of the Duke of Leeds. He was the vicar of the Dorset village of Durweston, which was in the gift of Lord Portman. He died in 1889, whereupon The Hive was inherited by his son, Sidney Francis Godolphin Osborne, one of H.M. Commissioners on the Board of the Inland Revenue, who was listed in the censuses of 1891 and 1901 as being at home there with his wife, Margaret, three sons and six staff.

The house was pulled down in the late 1950s and redeveloped as Hive Gardens, an estate of single-storey studio flats.

70. *Sandecotes Manor, between St Osmunds and Sandecotes Roads, which has been a school since 1893. For many years it was known as Uplands School, and today is the Bournemouth Collegiate Preparatory School.*

Sandecotes:

Sandecotes Road and St. Osmunds Road are first shown on the Greenwoods' map which was surveyed in 1825/6, and were on land owned by Canford Manor. The Sandecotes Estate lay largely between the two roads and consisted of a manor house set in about 75 acres of undulating woodland with fine views over Poole Harbour. In 1871 it was occupied by Edward Solly, his wife Alice and five daughters, and ten years later by Charles Forbes JP, who died there in 1887.

Lord Wimborne put the main part of the Sandecotes Estate up for sale by auction in London in September 1892, laid out with unmade roads and divided into plots for the development of individual houses. The estate then extended on both sides of Sandecotes Road, from Wellington Road and Belle Vue Roads in the north, and was bounded on the west and south by Alton Road, although several of the original road names (Belvedere, Guest, Sea View and Purbeck) have since been changed. Its elevated position gave houses here wide-ranging views over both the sea and the harbour, now largely obscured by the growth of trees.

In 1893, the Manor House was opened as the 'Bourne School for Girls at Sandecotes Manor', and two years later was extended by the construction of School House. In the census of 1901 it is listed as having 8 pupils between 12 and 17, with seven teaching and nine domestic staff. In 1900 it was given by Lady Wimborne to the Church Education Corporation, together with 2.5 acres of land. For many years it was simply known as 'Sandecotes School', and is the school described by Mary Butts of nearby Salterns House in her book 'The Crystal Cabinet'. During the Second World War the building was vacated by the school and used by the military. It is remembered by many people today as Uplands School, and

71. A postcard illustrating the interior of Sandecotes School in the early part of the 20th century.

72. A postcard showing the Sandecotes Estate in the early years of the 20th century, in course of development with substantial detached houses.

73. The view from the Sandecotes Estate in an early 20th century postcard, looking towards Poole town, with the chimneys of South Western Pottery standing prominently in the mid-ground.

is currently known as the Bournemouth Collegiate Preparatory School.

From the outset, the school needed a chapel and at first it was proposed to build this within the grounds. However the parish priest at St Peter's proposed a church open to the public and, with the help of the Wimbornes, a site was found for the first St Luke's, a prefabricated 'tin church'.

St. Luke's Church, Parkstone

74. The original "tin church", built about 1900 to serve the children of the Church Education Corporation's Sandecotes School, but also to be open to the public. It was soon to be replaced with St. Luke's Church in Wellington Road.

St Luke's became a separate parish in 1903 and the foundation stone for today's church was laid by Lady Wimborne in 1907. Although the fabric was completed by 1914, the First World War delayed its full completion until about 1920.

Castle Eve Estate:

There is mention of Castle Eve Villa in newspaper articles as far back as 1826, and the 1841 census records it as being occupied by Sophia Rowlett, a lady of independent means with three staff. It was a relatively modest house, set within a large site of perhaps fifty acres at the top of Castle Hill, to the south of the Bournemouth road. The house would have had magnificent views over Poole and the harbour. The estate was cut in two by the railway line when this was built between 1873-4, and the remaining land was then laid out with individual small building plots fronting Osborne, Sandringham, Balmoral, Windsor, Kingsbridge and Highmoor Roads.

Castle Eve is the estate that George Jennings, the owner of South Western Pottery, purchased in the 1860s as a family home for use when he was in Parkstone on holiday or visiting his pottery business He was resident there at the time of the Census in 1871 and is described as a *"Brick & pottery manufacturer employing 150 men and 20 boys; Farmer of 70 acres employing 8 men and 3 boys; and Shipowner employing 20 men"*. Living with him were his second wife, Sophia, aged 39, and children Catherine 31, Percy 8, Ethel 5, Florence 4 and Bertie 1, together with a cook, housemaid and nurse.

The Beehive Hotel:

There had been an inn on the Sandbanks Road near the salterns since the early 1800s, serving the salt workers, local farm hands and the occasional passing traveller. Originally belonging to Peregrine Baker, an early owner of Salterns House, it was purchased by Styring's Brewery in the 1860s, whose name can be seen in very faded paint on the facade in the earliest known photograph.

A few years later, Styrings entire business was acquired by the Dorchester brewers, Eldridge Pope, who continued to operate the Beehive until 1903, when they pulled down the old building and completely rebuilt it as The Beehive Hotel. The increasing attraction of Sandbanks as both a residential district and a weekend playground meant that there was

75. The brow of the hill leading down to Parkstone Village, after the Castle Eve Estate had been divided up into individual plots following George Jennings' death.

Castle Eve   Parkstone.

76. Judging by the raw state of the sides of the cutting, this very old picture dates from soon after the railway line was opened in 1874. It is taken from the heights of Castle Eve, looking back down the line to Parkstone Station and distant Poole.

a much greater passing trade and both the hotel element and the bars continued to flourish throughout the first half of the 20th century, justifying the addition of a new wing by 1920 and the subsequent acquisition of additional land. The Beehive remained the only proper pub in the whole area until it was demolished in 2001 to make way for 51 retirement flats.

As can be seen from period photographs of the Beehive, on the opposite side of the road was a schoolhouse, understood to have been built by George Jennings for the children of his pottery workers. Miss Mary Baker was the Schoolmistress for almost 30 years from the 1860s to the 1890s.

The final illustration in this chapter is of the Ordnance Survey map of 1890. This marks almost all the buildings described above, and makes it clear how much unspoilt countryside there was between each of them. But Parkstone-on-Sea would soon change beyond recognition.

77. The original Beehive Inn on the Sandbanks Road in 1890.

Andrew Hawks' Poole Picture Archive

78. In this postcard sent in 1905, the Beehive Hotel is pictured on the left, only recently rebuilt by the brewers, Eldridge Pope, in 1903. The schoolhouse is on the right, and the thatched cottage in the centre is on the corner of the drive to Salterns House, now Brownsea View Avenue.

79. This 1924 postcard shows the Beehive Hotel as a very comfortable establishment, still using the address 'Parkstone-on-Sea'. It has a tennis court, well-maintained gardens and the telephone number 'Canford Cliffs 9'.

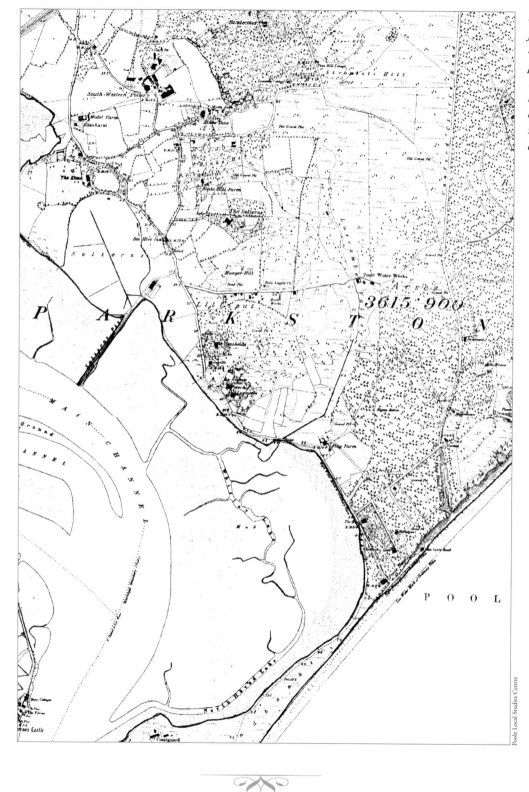

Poole Local Studies Centre

80. An extract from the Ordnance Survey map published in 1890 showing the locations of most of the buildings mentioned in this chapter.

Chapter 7

The Road to Sandbanks

What we know today as Sandbanks Road, in previous centuries called both Salterns Road and Brownsea Road, together with its continuation into Shore Road and Banks Road, has always been the principal thoroughfare through Parkstone-on-Sea. This turned off the main road from Poole across the heath to Christchurch, a short distance north of the town gates, and ran right down to North Haven Point at the end of the sandbanks. It has always been the main route to all the important buildings in the area – the salterns, the potteries, the large houses, the farms, the yacht clubs, the coalyard, the shipping wharf and the Beehive Inn.

For many of the early photographers in the first half of the 19th century this route provided a wide range of subjects for their large and unwieldy plate cameras, and many of the resultant photographs were published as postcards, sold to bring in an income. These still regularly come up for sale at postcard fairs today.

One prolific local photographer was Frederick Cathery, shown in the 1911 Census as living in Park View, Parkstone Village with his wife, Florence Mary, their daughter Doris

81. An advertisement in 'Parkstone Illustrated', a local guide book published by Cathery before WWI.

PARK VIEW STUDIO,
PARKSTONE.

COPIES OF THIS BOOK
POST FREE
TO ANY ADDRESS
SEVEN STAMPS.

FRED. CATHERY, M.P.P.A.,

PORTRAIT & LANDSCAPE PHOTOGRAPHER.

HIGH CLASS PHOTOGRAPHY AT MODERATE CHARGES.

Special Attention is given to Photographing Children. No effort spared to obtain Pleasing and Natural Results.

PRIVATE AND WEDDING GROUPS BY APPOINTMENT
OLD PHOTOGRAPHS, DRAWINGS, PAINTINGS, ETC., SUCCESSFULLY REPRODUCED.

PUBLISHER OF THE PARK VIEW SERIES OF LOCAL POST CARDS.

PHOTOGRAPHIC APPARATUS, PLATES, PAPERS, &c.
—— DARK ROOM. ——

4

aged eleven, and one servant. In about 1907, Frederick obviously walked the whole length of the Sandbanks Road, carrying his heavy camera and accompanied by Doris, who appears in many of the photographs, often with her bicycle.

Most of the following series of photographs date from between 1905 -1915, and many were taken by Frederick Cathery. They are arranged in sequence, as you come to them, walking down Sandbanks Road from Whitecliff, and continuing along Shore Road and then Banks Road as far as North Haven Point.

82. The Sandbanks Road, looking south-east towards the railway arch at Whitecliff, with Parkstone Farm on the right.

Poole Historical Trust

Sandbanks Road,   Parkstone

83. Whitecliff, taken from the site on which today stands the parade of shops containing Jones the butcher. Sandbanks Road crosses from left to right of the picture, with Salterns Road in the centre leading north to Ashley Cross.

84. Looking back along the Sandbanks Road towards Whitecliff. The large square house at the bend of the road is today Court's convenience store and the railway arch is out of sight around the bend in the road.

Valerie Sheldon

85. Edenhurst, a villa which had been built by George Jennings in about 1875 for members of his family. The bricks, drains, chimney pots, terracotta window surrounds and other ornamentation were all made within quarter of a mile at South Western Pottery.

Andrew Hawkes' Poole Picture Archive

The Road to Sandbanks

PARKSTONE SANDBANKS ROAD.

86. Sandbanks Road, opposite today's Whitecliff Playing Fields. On the left are cows grazing on land forming part of Jennings' Model Farm. The trees are shaped by the prevailing wind blowing in off Parkstone Bay.

"THE ELMS", PARKSTONE.

87. The gatehouse and main entrance to "The Elms", a small estate on land now occupied by Elms Avenue and Pearce Avenue. The drive enters very close to where Elms Close lies today.

88. Looking down the Sandbanks Road at the junction with Blake Hill Pottery Road, now known as Elgin Road. The Elms Estate is on the right.

Andrew Hawkes' Poole Picture Archive

89. The pair of 'Lady Wimborne cottages' which are still to be seen on the Sandbanks Road today, opposite the Elms Estate, although the barn behind them has now gone.

Andrew Hawkes' Poole Picture Archive

SANDBANKS R? PARKSTONE.

The Road to Sandbanks

90. *This postcard shows the thatched cottage situated next to the secondary drive into The Elms; a sign saying 'Tradesmen's Entrance' can be seen on the railings on the right. In the distance, a group of boys is sitting on the fence surrounding the lagoon.*

VIEW, SANDBANKS ROAD, PARKSTONE.

91. *The interior of the thatched cottage next to The Elms, with the elderly couple who lived there until the 1920s.*

Frank Henson

Chapter 7

92. A postcard taken looking back up the Sandbanks Road at the thatched cottage next to The Elms. Note the postman in his smart uniform and Doris with her bicycle. The railway lines which ran between South Western Pottery and Salterns Pier would have crossed the road just behind the camera.

93. Another postcard taken looking back up the Sandbanks Road, towards The Elms, with the lagoon behind the hedge on the left and fields on the right.

The Road to Sandbanks

94. *A short distance beyond The Elms lies a group of three buildings, the largest being The Beehive Hotel, on the right, which had been rebuilt on this site by Eldridge Pope in 1903.*

95. *The same location on Sandbanks Road, looking in the opposite direction. On the left is the Beehive Hotel, and on the right is the Schoolhouse, built by George Jennings for the children of his pottery workers. The thatched building in the centre is a staff cottage and coach-house on the corner of the driveway to Salterns House, now Brownsea View Avenue.*

96. A few yards off the Sandbanks Road, the view in this postcard was taken from behind the Beehive Hotel, looking across the lagoon towards The Elms estate, then almost entirely without trees. The outer breakwater of the lagoon is intact, and the water level is maintained by sluice gates which, at that time, were sited close to where the marina Inner Basin is today. The cows probably belong to Viney's Farm.

97. Salterns pier, with the lagoon on the left, and the rear of the Beehive Hotel beyond. In the centre is Jennings' coalyard building with its chimney, and the railway lines which led to South Western Pottery and Parkstone Station and were, by this time, little used. The area was to be regenerated as an industrial estate within a few years, at the start of the First World War.

VIEW FROM SALTERNS PIER, PARKSTONE.

The Road to Sandbanks

LILLIPUT HILL, PARKSTONE.

98. This postcard sent in 1909 shows four houses on Lord Alington's Lilliput Estate. That on the left is 'Evening Hill', which eventually gave its name to this part of the Sandbanks Road. Its site is now the Lewis-Manning Hospice.

99. At the bottom of Evening Hill was Whitley Pier, now used by East Dorset Sailing Club. This picture, taken from the end of the pier, shows some of the houses developed on Lord Alington's Lilliput Estate. The large mock-Tudor house is Lilliput House, rebuilt on this site in 1889 and still there today, divided into several dwellings.

Chapter 7   84

100. *The fields of Flag Farm are still free of development and the roadway remains unmetalled. The harbour wall, built in 1894 to protect Parkstone's newly-installed main outfall sewer and to stop the road being regularly washed away, is still there today. In this picture, the lamp standards have not yet got their lamps.*

101. *A solitary cyclist contemplates the harbour over the recently-built sea wall in front of Flag Farm. Cows belonging to the farm can be seen in the background, together with some of the substantial villas on the Lilliput Estate.*

THE SEA WALL, PARKSTONE-ON-SEA.

85   The Road to Sandbanks

102. The Sandbanks Road has now merged into Shore Road and, although increasing numbers of new villas are now to be seen on the Lilliput Estate, transport was still only by horse or on foot.

103. This photograph, taken close to the junction of Shore Road and Banks Road, illustrates how many trees had been planted to transform the original bare heathland. The telegraph poles carry the lines serving The Haven Hotel.

104. These Edwardian ladies, possibly nannies or governesses out for a walk with their charges, suggest that Sandbanks had started to become a popular place for well-to-do families. Behind the wall on the left is Lord Osborne's house "The Hive", the site of today's Hive Gardens. Amongst the trees, occupying a large site between Shore Road and Banks Road, is "Sand Acres", the seaside retreat of Sir Ernest Cassel, grandfather of Lady Mountbatten. It is now part of the Sandbanks Hotel.

105. An early postcard showing the three buildings marked on Barnes' map of 1895, at the junction of today's Shore Road and Haven Road. The large house is Sand Acres, belonging to Sir Ernest Cassel, which now forms part of the Sandbanks Hotel.

106. This postcard, postmarked 1907, shows Sandbanks with very little obvious development apart from two houses almost opposite the castle on Brownsea Island. The "road" appears to run along the beach fronting the harbour.

Sandbanks & Brownsea.

107. Following the sale of building plots in 1896 by Poole Harbour Commissioners, who had acquired most of Sandbanks from Lord Wimborne, houses gradually started to be built fronting the beach. In the distance amongst the trees can be seen two of the earliest houses, The Hive and Sand Acres.

HAVEN ROAD SANDBANKS

108. A postcard sent in 1913 showing one of the early houses fronting the beach on what is now Banks Road. The groynes constructed by the Harbour Commissioners to prevent the sea breaching the neck of the sandbanks can clearly be seen.

109. The Haven Hotel was built in 1880. This picture, used in an advertisement of 1906, shows that due to the success of the business, the original building has been considerably extended.

This series of photographs, following the road from Whitecliff to the tip of Sandbanks, gives a good impression of what Parkstone-on-Sea was like one hundred years ago, as the 20th century dawned. There were significant pockets of industry, particularly South Western Pottery and around the salterns, and several small brickworks. In addition to the few original important houses, increasing numbers of large seaside villas or "summer houses" were being built on the Lilliput and Flag Farm estates, as well as at Canford Cliffs and on the sandbanks themselves. Much of the rest of Parkstone-on-Sea remained rural - peaceful woods and farmland.

The Road to Sandbanks

Poole Local Studies Centre

110. Poole's first lifeboat, the Manley Wood, pictured in about 1870 on a fund-raising tour of Bournemouth. This was stationed on the 'remote headland' of sandbanks from 1865.

111. The Coastguard Station, cottages and Harbour House, taken soon after 1900, before the construction of any other buildings on the harbour shore of Sandbanks.

Andrew Hawkes' Poole Picture Archive

Chapter 8

Chapter 8:

The Sandbanks

Until the end of the 19th century, there was still no such place as 'Sandbanks', with a capital 'S'. There were indeed the sandbanks which separated Poole Harbour from the open sea, terminating in North Haven Point by the harbour entrance, but no-one lived there. There was a Coastguard Station on the northern shore, a wooden gamekeeper's hut on the approach to the narrowest part and perhaps a few temporary fisherman's shelters, but there were no roads and the landscape was wild and totally undeveloped. Shooting parties of wildfowlers were occasional visitors, and towards the end of the century, adventurous picnickers might make a day trip by boat from Poole Quay.

Poole's first lifeboat, the "Manley Wood" was housed on the *"remote headland"* of North Haven Point in 1865. This was a pulling boat with 10 oarsmen who first had to assemble at the Antelope in Poole to be taken by horse-drawn cart to the sandbanks to launch the boat. The Coxswain was Richard Stokes, who doubled as a Coastguard and as light keeper for Trinity House, for whom he maintained the leading lights which guided vessels into the harbour in the dark. He later had what was described as a *"very commodious"* house built for him, and Stokes' Cottage still exists in Old Coastguard Road today, although it is doubtful whether he would recognise it! In the same road still stands a row of terraced cottages, built in 1876 to house the staff of the Coastguard station, although the separate house for their officer has since disappeared. The lifeboat station was moved from the sandbanks to the eastern end of Poole Quay in 1882, where its purpose-built boathouse can still be seen.

112. An advertisement for the Haven Hotel published in 1896. It shows that the original building has already been extended substantially, but Mr Witherington is at least the third proprietor since it opened in 1880. Note the address: Parkstone-on-Sea.

In the late 1870s, a Mr Peter Tuck submitted plans to Poole Council, seeking permission to build a new hotel at the very tip of North Haven Point. Initially these plans were refused on the grounds that he proposed to discharge the drainage directly into the sea, and

91   The Sandbanks

consent was only granted after this was changed to a cesspit. This was ironic because, barely 20 years later when Parkstone got its own public drainage system, the main sewer outfall was laid all the way down the Sandbanks Road, along the edge of the harbour, and discharged the entire district's untreated contents directly into the sea off Shore Road!

The Haven Hotel opened in 1880. It was a brave move, because there was no proper road access; the unsurfaced Sandbanks Road petered out before you got to the peninsular, and from here a pedestrian track led along the harbour shore and then inland across the sand dunes to North Haven Point. Business may initially have been slow because within a year Mr Tuck had let the premises fully furnished and equipped, and the 1881 Census lists the proprietor as an Irishman, John Odlum, with his wife and daughter. They employed a chambermaid, waiter, a male general servant and a child aged eight. However the hotel gradually built up a very successful business, most particularly when a 30 year old French hotelier, Eugine Poulain, took over in 1899 with his Canadian-born wife, Francis Anne.

113. The proprietor of the Haven Hotel, Monsieur Poulain, seated in one of his fleet of De Dion Bouton charabancs outside the hotel about 1910.

Poole Local Studies Centre

The Poulains ran a fleet of magnificent De Dion Bouton charabancs to transport the hotels clientele, who included many Royal and titled guests, the poet Robert Browning and other more ordinary mortals just seeking peace, quiet and excellent food. The family also ran motor launches to ferry their guests to Shell Bay, Studland and Poole, and continued to manage the hotel until about 1918.

From 1898, the Marquis Guglielmo Marconi used the hotel as a base to carry out his pioneering research into the development of radio, and for almost 30 years the hotel was adorned with his array of aerials. His elegant steam yacht, Elettra, was often to be seen anchored in Brownsea Roads.

Towards the end of the 19th century, a number of factors combined to change the nature of this remote headland beyond recognition. The prosperity of Poole has always depended upon its maritime trade. A significant hindrance to this trade was the sand bar off the entrance which limited the draught of vessels able to enter the harbour. This bar was caused by sand which had been swept westward by the tide along the beaches of Poole Bay and settled at the mouth of the harbour; the harbour's outgoing tidal flow scoured the actual entrance but, as it slowed down, the bar formed about a mile out. Since the mid 1700s, a succession of engineers' reports had been commissioned by Poole Council on how to overcome the

problem; they all said broadly the same thing: a stone 'training bank' should be built on one side of the harbour entrance, extending some distance out to sea, to speed up the flow of the outgoing water to scour out the bar.

Each time the Council looked with horror at the cost of the work and either did not have, or did not want to spend, the money to remedy the problem. The bar remained and, as ships got larger throughout the Victorian era, the adverse affect on Poole's trade got even worse.

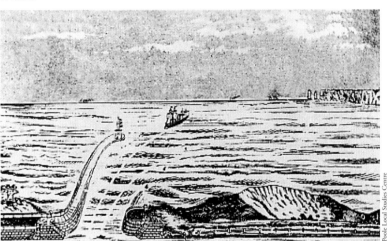

115. A copy of an oil painting in Poole Museum, commissioned by a Mr Joyner in the 1860s in an attempt to persuade Poole Council to cut a new entrance to the harbour through the neck of the sandbanks, so avoiding the bar which prevented large ships entering.

Throughout the 1800s there were regular pleas to Poole Council to do something to improve the access to the harbour over the bar. Deputations from local traders, petitions from the Bournemouth Chamber of Trade and other local trade associations, as well as requests from the operators of shipping, all had little effect. One particularly vociferous local trader was a Mr. Joyner, who put forward a plan to change the harbour's entrance completely, cutting through the neck of the sandbanks in a direct line from the North Channel and damming the existing entrance, so the tide had a more direct line to the Quay. He even went as far as to commission an oil painting of his proposal, in an endeavour to convince the Council. However, inertia continued to rule: one reason was that matters relating to the Harbour Committee were traditionally the last items on the Agenda for the monthly Council Meetings and so, by the time they came up for consideration, many of the Council Members had got their coats on to go home. Harbour issues were rarely considered a priority.

By about 1890, the scouring of the beaches at the sandbanks had become so severe that the neck of the peninsular was reduced to only 40 yards wide in places. There was real concern that the sea would break through, turning the sandbanks into an island and causing such a reduction in the flow of water through the Haven that the main harbour entrance would silt up. This would have been a disaster for Poole's trade. The independent engineer advising the Council, a Mr Kinipple, recommended that longer groynes should be built on the sea shore to intercept the flow of sand and so build up the beach again.

The sandbanks were by this time once again owned by Canford Manor, and it took four years of negotiation and many deputations of Councillors out to Canford to meet Lord Wimborne before agreement was reached as to the terms on which groynes could be erected on his land. In fact, Lord Wimborne was anxious to avoid the responsibility of paying for sea defence works, and eventually it was agreed that he would give all of the sandbanks to the Council, with the exception of those sites such as the Haven Hotel and the Coastguard Station which had already been sold off; the Manor would retain only that land (now in Panorama Road) which had water frontage to the harbour. Historians disagree about whether, and if so how much, consideration changed hands in this transaction, but certainly the Council then assumed responsibility for building and subsequently maintaining the sea defence works.

116. Ivor Guest, 1st Baron Wimborne, who was Lord of the Manor at Canford Magna from 1852 – 1914, although his wife, Lady Cornelia, continued to live there until 1922.

Whilst all this was going on, the authority of Poole Council to run the harbour was being challenged by a group of disgruntled merchants and harbour users who were tired of the decades of inaction over the problem of the bar, and of being charged harbour dues by a body on which they had no representation. In 1894 they formed the 'Merchants Association of Poole' to press for direct representation on the Harbour Committee. When this was refused, the Association submitted a private Bill to Parliament, with the object of transferring the duties of harbour management from the Council to an independent Harbour Board, of whom half were to be harbour users, elected by those who paid £5 or more in harbour dues.

Of course, Poole Council objected to the Bill, which was referred to a Select Committee of the House of Lords for a decision. The Council's case was not helped by its own Consulting Engineer saying in evidence that Poole "*has been one of the most backward places in the kingdom for harbour improvements*"! The Select Committee unanimously recommended that the Bill should become law as the Poole Harbour Act 1895, creating a new independent body to manage the harbour, with equal representation on it from the Council and harbour users. However the Council was theoretically given a voting majority by the stipulation that the Mayor should always be the Chairman.

The new "Commissioners for the Harbour of Poole" assumed their responsibilities for the management of the harbour on the 9th November 1895, and immediately inherited both Poole Quay and the sandbanks (parts of which they still own today) together with the necessity of building the groynes. It was how to raise the money to pay for these works that caused the first friction between the new body of Commissioners and the Corporation from which it had just parted.

Although the make-up of the Harbour Commissioners was drawn equally from the Corporation and commerce, in fact a number of the Councillors also had business interests in the harbour and its trade, so there was a majority prepared to take a hard-nosed commercial approach to running the harbour. To raise the money for the sea defences, they proposed to divide the sandbanks up into building plots and to sell them off. They created a 'Groynes Sub-committee' which commissioned a detailed survey of the land, and a plan for its future development, from a local surveyor, Mr H. F. J. Barnes. This plan, and the proposal to sell off 40 plots, was discussed at a full meeting of the Commissioners reported in the Bournemouth Guardian in May 1896. A majority was in favour, but the Mayor protested strongly against the whole of the land at the sandbanks being laid out in building sites. He believed that *the one great object in taking it over was to keep it as an open space*; it was *the lungs of Poole and to build upon it would be an absolute disaster for the town*.

The Commissioners' response to the Mayor's appeal was uncompromising: they said it was not their intention to build over the whole of the land, but *the sandbanks was the only available asset they had, and they should get as much out of it as they could* to recoup the money to be spent on the groynes. They felt that the excursionists who came to picnic only used the beaches and it was not proposed to build on those. *If it was the desire of the Town to have open spaces in the sandbanks, the Council might purchase any of the plots it liked and keep them for that purpose*. The motion to sell 40 plots at auction was carried.

117. An advertisement in the Bournemouth Guardian of 30th May 1896 for the forthcoming auction on behalf of the Harbour Commissioners of building plots on the sandbanks.

The Commissioners then instructed two local firms of Auctioneers jointly to offer the plots for sale on the basis of an annual Ground Rent, with the option of subsequently buying the Freehold. The auction was held at the Antelope Hotel in Poole on 18th June 1896 and 17 of the 40 plots were sold at Ground Rents ranging between £4 and £5.10s per annum. The leases provided that, once a house to the value of £400 had been erected by the Lessee, he could then purchase the Freehold for 25 times the Ground Rent, so in effect, the plots were selling at between £100 and £125. In the next few years the remainder of the plots were sold off, with the exception of the large site where the Corporation's Pavilion and Beach Huts now stand, which was conveyed to the Council in 1905 – whether it had to pay for it has not been established.

Almost every long-term Poole resident seems to have a family myth that *"Grandfather could have bought all of Sandbanks for £5"* or £50 or even £500. It is difficult to understand how there could be any truth in these stories. It is, of course, possible that, before 1895, Lord Wimborne would have been happy to sell the sandbanks for a fairly nominal sum, but the new landowner would have had to carry out the sea defence works at his own expense

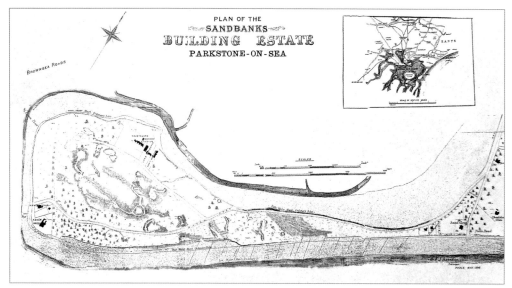

118. The survey of the sandbanks undertaken in 1895 by Mr HFJ Barnes for the Harbour Commissioners, showing the buildings already existing at that time, but as yet without his proposals for dividing the land into building plots.

– the total cost would not have amounted to a bargain price! After 1895, the sandbanks belonged to the newly-formed Harbour Commissioners, who were intent on maximising the sale proceeds from the building plots to pay for the sea defence works, and would not have been in the least interested in selling cheaply.

The map of the sandbanks prepared in 1896 by Mr Barnes on the instructions of the new Harbour Commissioners is interesting because it shows which buildings already existed at that time. There weren't many: on the tip of North Haven Point was the Haven Hotel, opened in 1880. Next to it was a private house, Haven Villa, built a few years after the hotel. By the 1950s this had become the Ferry Cafe, and the Golden Gates block of flats is now built on the site.

Fronting the harbour, opposite Branksea Island, was the row of Coastguard Cottages and their boathouse, next to which was Harbour View House built by Lord Wimborne, which later became Harvey's Tea Rooms and now lies beneath the Royal Motor Yacht Club boatshed. This adjoined a range of buildings consisting of a coach-house, stabling and staff

Frank Henson

119. Harbour View House built by Lord Wimborne, and the coach-house and stabling belonging to the owners of Branksea Island, taken from the harbour shore. The gable end of the row of Coastguard cottages can just be seen on the right of the picture.

120. Sand Acres, built in the late 1880s adjacent to Poole Head by Sir Ernest Cassel as a holiday home by the sea. It was used as a military convalescent home during the First World War, and now forms part of the Sandbanks Hotel.

121. A postcard sent in 1907, showing some of the temporary huts on the sandbanks, many put up without any permission or any services. Amongst the trees in the background can be seen The Hive and Sand Acres.

accommodation belonging to the owner of Branksea (now Brownsea) Island who, at that time, was Captain Kenneth Balfour. When, in 1900, the island was purchased by Charles van Raalte, he improved the access road for his carriages – this would later be known as Panorama Road. It was the ownership of these buildings on the mainland of Poole that enabled Mr van Raalte to accept the position of Mayor in 1902.

At the other end of the peninsula had been built a small group of early houses, just under the cliff known as Poole Head, and close to Chaddesley Glen. The largest of these was a substantial Victorian house called Sand Acres, built as a seaside villa by Sir Ernest Cassel, close friend and banker to the Prince of Wales (later King Edward VII) and grandfather of Lady Edwina Mountbatten. The garden included the whole triangular site between Shore Road and Banks Road, and its staff cottage is now the site of the current Sandacres flats and Tesco Express. During the First World War, it was used as a Convalescent Home for injured officers and remained in the family until after Sir Ernest's death in 1921. The original house has been vastly extended and is almost entirely swallowed up by the Sandbanks Hotel, but its gable end can still be identified on the elevation fronting the beach.

Next to Sand Acres were two smaller dwellings, one called 'The Bungalow', and just a few yards further west, fronting the harbour shore, was another of the very early houses. 'The Hive' was a substantial house built in the 1850s as a summer retreat for Lord Osborne, the vicar of Durweston in Dorset. This was redeveloped in the 1960s as Hive Gardens, but the original Victorian sea wall can still be seen fronting Shore Road, a few yards east of Chaddesley Glen.

Apart from these early buildings, as the 19th century came to a close, the peninsular was still a wild and largely uninhabited place, although gradually a number of temporary huts began to be put up in the dunes and along the beach by picnickers wanting a more substantial base for their excursions. These had no facilities or sanitation and eventually many of them were compulsorily cleared away. Mary Butts of Salterns House recalls *"the sandbanks in my childhood was a pale sand and couch-grass wilderness, honeycombed with rabbits; and the tallest dune, High Horse Manger, a two hundred foot slide on a tea tray into the soft, pure, drift at its foot"*.

In 1898 a new pier was built at North Haven Point by Captain Balfour of Branksea Island, and was opened by the Mayor. This was almost 100 feet long and, as well as improving access to the island, allowed steamships, particularly the paddle-steamers, to include Sandbanks in their itinerary of Poole Quay, Bournemouth Pier and, later, Swanage and brought many more day trippers to enjoy the beaches.

A tram service between Poole and County Gates had opened in about 1901, which was soon joined to the Bournemouth network. Then in 1904 there was a proposal by the 'Bournemouth, Parkstone, Studland & Swanage Light Railway Company' to lay tramlines to Sandbanks and then continue the service on to Studland and Swanage by means of a 'transporter bridge', 90 feet high across the harbour entrance. Despite the fact that the principal shareholders in the company were major landowners, including Lord Wimborne,

123. A postcard sent in 1917, but probably photographed some ten years earlier, showing a large party of day-trippers or 'excursionists' enjoying the beach fronting the harbour at Sandbanks, in front of Harvey's Tea Rooms.

124. A photograph from about 1911 showing the recently constructed Grasmere and Seacombe Roads, with three houses, North Haven House with its guest bungalow, Byfleet and Cama, standing alone on the harbour shore. It illustrates very clearly why the area was called the sandbanks!

Sir John Burt of Swanage and Mr Bankes of Kingston Lacey who owned Studland, there was strong opposition, including from Sandbanks residents, who feared an increase in 'excursionists' of an unsuitable type! An enquiry by The Commissioners for Light Railways in 1906 eventually rejected the proposals. One further attempt to bridge the entrance was made in 1929, this time by the company which owned the chain ferry, which submitted a Bill to Parliament for the construction of a toll bridge 105 feet off the water, approached by a spiral ramp on the Sandbanks side. It was strongly opposed by both Poole Council and the Harbour Commissioners, but was defeated in the House of Commons by only four votes.

After the auction of building plots by the Harbour Commissioners in 1896, roads

125. A postcard from about 1910 showing some of the houses built on Sandbanks following the sale of building plots by the Harbour Commissioners. On the left, by the harbour shore, is one of the earliest houses, Bay View, where the Bay View shops are today.

were constructed and more substantial dwellings began to be built, and the development of what had now become "Sandbanks" with a capital "S" was well under way. By 1903, most of the road pattern we would recognise today was in place, although not yet tarmacadamed, and by the time of the First World War, a scattering of small houses had sprung up amongst the dunes. At this stage, few of the dwellings were of much substance except, perhaps, North Haven House, and another called Bay View which stands where the parade of shops is today. Indeed many were of very modest construction, including a selection of what could only be described as temporary timber buildings, and at least one converted railway carriage remained among the dunes until the late 1950s. As Sandbanks developed, many successful and wealthy people built or bought homes among the dunes, often as holiday homes, but

126. A postcard sent in 1913 (but probably taken rather earlier) showing one of the earliest houses fronting on to Sandbanks beach. It confirms that the groynes constructed by the Harbour Commissioners to prevent the neck of the peninsular being breached by the sea are proving effective in building up sand on the shore. [6.17]

127. Edwardian picnickers enjoy a weekend in their tent "at the sandbanks", with more substantial dwellings in the background.

Andrew Hawkes' Poole Picture Archive

128. In the centre of this photograph is North Haven House, built by Frederick and Emmeline Toms in 1905. The 3 acre site on Panorama Road extended from the tennis court on the right to include Byfleet, the house and stabling at the rear, and the chalet bungalow for guests. The latter is still there today, in the ownership of the same family.

Jon Hooker

occasionally as their principal residence. These included , in the early days, Lord Leonard Lyle MP, Chairman of Tate & Lyle; later, Billy Cotton the band leader; and today there is Harry Redknapp, the football manager. Most of these have come and gone again, but there are at least four families whose predecessors built homes here in the early part of the century and their descendants have remained loyal to Sandbanks for five or more generations.

The first of these, and almost certainly the longest established on Sandbanks, is the Toms family. Frederick Toms, a silk merchant from Epsom, and his wife Emmeline came to Sandbanks in the very early years of the 20th century, buying from Lord Wimborne a three acre site on Panorama Road on which they built 'North Haven House'. This was a substantial home with eight bedrooms, three reception rooms and 'complete domestic offices', completed in 1905. Within the grounds was a separate chalet-bungalow for guests, and the Toms' daughter, Madeleine, built a house next door called 'Byfleet' which was to be destroyed by a German bomb in 1942.

Frederick had become very ill, and it is likely that his move to Sandbanks was because his doctor recommended bracing sea air. He died at North Haven House in May 1907, aged only 52, but Emmeline continued to live there until her own death in August 1941. A sale of the main house had to wait until after the war, but it was offered at auction by Fox & Sons in July 1946 and redeveloped with four new houses. However the family kept the original guest house at 106 Panorama Road and it is still today the home of Emmeline and Frederick's great-grandson, Jon Hooker, who himself has children and grandchildren – six generations of this family have enjoyed Sandbanks. Jon has other interesting ancestors: on his paternal side, another great-grandfather was Sir Joseph Dalton Hooker, the great Victorian botanist, plant collector and friend of Darwin, who was Director of Kew Gardens from 1865 - 1885.

Sandbanks.

Andrew Hawkes' Poole Picture Archive

129. Haven Road (now Banks Road) just before the First World War. Ebb Tide is opposite Brownsea Road, which goes off to the right, and in the distance is the Haven Hotel with Marconi's radio mast showing clearly.

In 1915, Percy and Isabelle Allen from Westbury on Trim in Gloucestershire paid £500 for 'Ebb Tide' a house built about 1905 at 151 Banks Road, close to the Haven Hotel. Although formally referring to himself as 'director of a printing company', much of Percy's income apparently derived from weekly visits to London gambling clubs where he played a largely successful game of Poker. Nobody knows what brought him to Sandbanks, but there is a family suspicion that the purchase was the result of a winning night at the gaming table. Today Ebb Tide is owned by two of his grandsons and, despite having to fend off frequent approaches by developers, they continue to enjoy regular holidays in what is one of the last of the original beach-front houses. The sixth generation of the Allen family is now enjoying Sandbanks, as the house approaches 100 years in their ownership.

Another family with a long established connection with Sandbanks is the Yeatmans, an old-established Dorset family of lawyers and millers, who have had premises on Poole Quay for many generations. Archibald Yeatman bought a large plot at 83 Banks Road, on the neck of the peninsular, in 1920. On this he built a modest timber bungalow for family beach holidays which, in typical Sandbanks fashion, stood as a marked contrast to its neighbour, a very grand house called 'Storm', built by Lady Kemnel. Although Archibald was sadly killed in an accident off the beach in 1932, when he struck his head on a rock, the little bungalow passed to his brother Neville and then down his line to today's generation. In 1979, they came to an arrangement with a developer who replaced the wooden bungalow with a block of flats, of which Anthony Yeatman and his family retain the penthouse. Their children and grandchildren are still enjoying the beaches of Sandbanks today.

The largest family with a long and continuing connection with Sandbanks is the one about whom there are the most misconceptions: the Andreaes. They came from an old-established family of Lutheran merchants and bankers from Northern Germany who had moved to England early in the Victorian era. They were closely linked to the

130. The Andreae children, known as the 'Straight Eight', photographed in the garden of 'Merricot' in Banks Road in 1938. The only boy, John, came in at No.7!

131. Dr Eddie Andreae and his wife Constance on the beach at Sandbanks in 1928.

Kleinwort banking family, both through business and by marriage, and one brother, Herman Andreae, joined the London merchant bank, Kleinwort Sons & Co, in 1897, becoming Chairman in 1948. He was a keen yachtsman and member of the Royal Yacht Squadron, racing the 23 metre *Candida* which he built in 1928 and subsequently buying the J Class *Endeavour* from Sir Tommy Sopwith in 1935. Family legend has it that he had sailed into Poole Harbour and subsequently told his brother, Eddie, that he had found the most delightful place called Sandbanks where he suggested he should take his ever-growing brood of children for summer holidays.

That brother, Dr. Edward Andreae PhD, was not a banker but an industrial chemist. He was Chairman of the British subsidiary of a German company with a factory in Flint which developed and manufactured an early synthetic fibre, rayon. He negotiated a highly beneficial take-over by the manufacturing giant, Courtauld, which secured the start of his fortune. His particular skill, however, was as what we would call today a 'company doctor': taking failing companies and nursing them back into profitability before selling them on at a profit. Acting on his brother's advice, he first came to Sandbanks with his wife, Constance and three children, for a summer holiday in a rented bungalow in 1919. They liked it so much that in 1920 he bought Kootenays in Banks Road which he extended substantially and renamed Merricot, and this is still owned by descendants to this day.

Between 1915 and 1929, Eddie and Constance Andreae had eight children, all but the seventh, John, being girls. The whole family loved the beaches, the boating and the freedom which Sandbanks offered for summer holidays and, as their children grew and eventually married and had their own children, so Dr Andreae bought or built more houses

132. The junction of Banks Road with Panorama Road in the mid 1930s, now apparently with a concrete surface. The little chapel of St Nicholas was consecrated in 1930, and the shops and houses of the Bay View Estate were developed in 1932.

to accommodate them all. These were all held in a Family Trust controlled by him and, by the late 1960s, this owned an unbroken line of six homes overlooking Sandbanks beach, No's 111-121 Banks Road, together with No.135 and four houses on the other side of Banks Road. Dr Andrea also contributed substantially to the cost of the little wooden Chapel of St Nicholas, consecrated in 1930.

On the death of Dr Andreae in 1975, all the properties had to be sold out of the trust, many being purchased by the family members who used them. The trust, however, still exists and, with over 100 members, owns one of the most extraordinary properties to have survived in today's glitzy, densely-developed Sandbanks. Coveted by every developer, the Boatshed at 16 Panorama Road, with its long frontage to the harbour shore, is a reminder of what Sandbanks used to be like, undeveloped except for a small cottage, a tennis court and a modern industrial building used for boat storage. Today it forms the focus for summer holidays for the extended family, a large number of whom gather on Sandbanks every August, although only a few still bear the Andreae name – with seven sisters, it was left to the only boy to carry that on.

The building of new homes on Sandbanks continued slowly but steadily after the First World War, and was boosted by the opening of the chain ferry to South Haven Point in 1926 and the improvements to the main road funded by a Government scheme to provide work for the unemployed. The area continued to attract memorable characters, and others have recounted in more detail the story of the redoubtable Miss Louie Foott (later Mrs Dingwall) who started a bus service from Sandbanks using a converted Model T Ford. She became one of the very first women to be licensed by the resolutely male Jockey Club as a racehorse trainer, with stables in Panorama Road, and training gallops along the beach.

Poole Corporation opened the Sandbanks Pavilion and beach huts in 1928, designed by the Borough Engineer and Surveyor, Ernest Goodacre on the site it had owned since 1905. This increased the facilities for day-trippers, but shopping for residents was slow to appear.

133. The original steam-driven chain ferry was opened in 1926, enabling vehicles to cross the harbour mouth for the first time. An attempt by the operating company to claim a monopoly on all passengers was defeated in the courts, allowing the traditional fierce rivalry between the Harvey's and Davis's passenger launches to continue for further generations.

134. The main road through Sandbanks in the 1920s, which was made-up following the opening of the ferry, using a Government-sponsored scheme to give work to the unemployed. Then known as Haven Road, it is now called Banks Road. On the right is the house, Bay View, where the shops are today.

135. The first shop and Post Office on Sandbanks opened in about 1923 in Panorama Road. It also did good business as a cafe.

Several enterprising shopkeepers from Parkstone took the opportunity to fill this void, one of whom had a van fitted out as a mobile greengrocers which he would slowly drive around the unmade roads, and another would cycle down to take grocery orders for delivery the next day. The first local shop, cafe and Post Office opened in Panorama Road, close to its junction with Banks Road, in the mid 1920s, and this was followed

The Sandbanks

136. The north shore of Sandbanks in 1930. Centre foreground is the terrace of Coastguard Cottages with the original lifeboat house in front. Beyond that is the boathouse of the Haven Launch Company with Harbour View House at the rear; this was demolished when Lord Lyle extended the boatshed for use by the Poole Harbour Yacht Company. Much land remains undeveloped.

137. A yacht hauled out at the boatyard of the Poole Harbour Yacht Company on the north shore of Sandbanks in the mid 1930s.

by the parade of shops which is still there today, built on the site of one of the earliest houses, called Bay View.

Sandbanks also had its commercial users, principally in the form of boatyards. The first half of the large boatshed which now belongs to RMYC was built on the garden of Harbour View House in about 1929 by Reginald Collis for his Haven Launch Company, but this was wound up in 1931. It was then bought by Lord Lyle who extended the shed for the use of his Poole Harbour Yacht Company Ltd, and a little further along the harbour shore was the boatyard of the Sandbanks Yacht Company; both of these yards had facilities to haul out quite substantial yachts. Just off the harbour shore in Witley Lake appeared a number of houseboats, some used only temporarily as floating beach huts, others occupied permanently. Although this seemed a romantic concept, the authorities had grave concerns over their sanitary arrangements and eventually they were moved compulsorily to Bramble Bush Bay on South Haven Point. Only five remain today.

138. A postcard sent in 1928 showing some of the houseboats permanently moored in Witley Lake on the northern shore of Sandbanks. These were eventually required to move to the other side of the harbour entrance, due to concerns over their sanitary arrangements.

139. The new pier and clubhouse of The Royal Motor Yacht Club at Sandbanks, soon after it opened in 1936. The adjoining boathouse was acquired from the Poole Harbour Yacht Company at a later date.

The Royal Motor Yacht Club opened its brand new clubhouse in Panorama Road in 1936. Founded in 1905 as the motor-boating arm of the Royal Automobile Club, it had been based for some years in a converted yacht called Florinda, tied to Poole Quay. The Commodore learned that Phyllis Lee-Duncan, the owner of the Royal Bath Hotel in Bournemouth, was building a block of two large flats on a site with harbour frontage, next to the yard of Poole Harbour Yacht Company. She was persuaded to sell the entire property and the plans were amended to provide a dining room, bar, billiard room, 17 single cabins with bunk beds and ancillary offices. A new pier gave access at all states of the tide. That clubhouse is still there today.

The 1930s on Sandbanks are remembered by residents and visitors alike as an idyllic period, a period of happy informal holidays and messing about in boats. This was to change dramatically at the end of the decade when its beaches were fortified by the military as the front line against an expected invasion by Nazi troops.

140. By the late 1930s the beach on the northern shore of Sandbanks was packed with small boats, and dozens more lay on moorings just offshore. All these would have to be cleared away when war was declared in September 1939.

Chapter 9

Canford Cliffs

The area we know today as Canford Cliffs, between Poole Head and Canford Cliffs Chine, is marked on 18th century maps as 'Mines Heath'. The only sign of habitation at that time was a single clifftop house owned by Mr Ralph Willets of Merley House; otherwise it was part of the barren and virtually treeless heathland which stretched as far as Christchurch. Although never really regarded part of Parkstone-on-Sea, Canford Cliffs was originally part of Canford Manor, lay within the Tything of Parkstone, and formed part of the Haven Estate acquired by Nicholas Mead in 1610. It passed down into the possession of the Cload family and was sold off by their executors in about 1768. The Sturt family of Crichel bought Flag Farm, and it seems that much of the remainder of the estate, excluding the sandbanks, was purchased by the Webb family of Canford Manor, who had failed to regain possession of the Haven Estate in a court action in 1745.

141. Branksome Tower, the mansion built by Charles Packe in the mid 1850s, on the clifftop of the Branksome Park Estate, above Branksome Chine.

By the second half of the 19th century, a number of factors had come together to suggest to landowners in Parkstone that housing development might be successful. Most important was the growth of the new seaside resort of Bournemouth only three miles to

Andrew Hawkes' Poole Picture Archive

Andrew Hawkes' Poole Picture Archive

142. The Martello tower overlooking Canford Cliffs Chine, built as a folly by the owner of Branksome Tower. It is photographed in the 1870s when it was the only building visible on this part of the coast.

the east. This was becoming increasingly popular based on its claims of a mild climate, pure sea air and the perceived health-giving properties of the pine trees planted in their millions by estate owners and early developers. The National TB Sanatorium opened in 1855, the first pier in 1861 and the railway arrived in 1870, greatly improving the accessibility of the whole area.

Another factor was the exclusive 750 acre Branksome Park Estate which lay between Bournemouth and Canford Cliffs and which undoubtedly influenced the development of neighbouring land. This was initially the home of Charles Packe, MP for South Leicestershire, who had bought the estate in 1853 and built a substantial mansion, Branksome Tower. After the death of his wife in 1870, it was sold to Henry Bury (pronounced 'Burry'), a banker from Manchester, who retained 250 acres around Branksome Tower itself and laid out the road pattern to enable the rest of the estate to be divided into large building plots. Bury lived here for only a short time until his death in 1876, after which the remainder of the estate became available for development as well. The mansion, with nine acres of land, was converted into one of the country's most prestigious hotels and was eventually redeveloped with flats and houses in the 1970s.

Although Charles Packe is today largely forgotten, he leaves a legacy in the shape of the family mausoleum at the head of Branksome Dene Chine and in the names of the roads on his estate. Particularly Martello Park and Martello Road refer to the massive stone tower which he built on the cliff top overlooking Canford Cliffs Chine. This was a folly which is marked as the "Martello Tower" at the very south-western corner of the Estate maps, as well as on 19th century maritime charts, and on the Ordnance Survey

143. The beach below the Canford Cliffs, stretching from Poole Head on the left, with Sand Acres just visible, past Flaghead Chine to Canford Cliffs Chine in the distance where the Martello Tower can be seen.

maps between 1893 and the 1920s. However, sometime before 1930, cliff erosion toppled it on to the beach, where no trace now remains.

Immediately to the west of Branksome Park, above a superb beach and with 2000 feet of frontage to the clifftop between Canford Cliffs Chine and Poole Head, lay an area of heathland which was to become known as the Canford Cliffs Estate. Since the Canford Manor Inclosure Award of 1807, this had been owned in two separate parts of almost equal size: the western half extending to some 60 acres was retained by Lord de Mauley, when he sold the rest of Canford Manor to the Guests in 1847. In 1861, de Mauley sold this land to his first cousin, Lord Bessborough, for £1,500, and three years later it was bought for £2,000 by potential developers, the West Bournemouth Land & Cliff Hotel Company Ltd. represented by a Poole solicitor, Martin Kemp Welch. Whatever its development plans were, they failed, and in May 1868 the company was put into liquidation at the petition of a creditor, George Jennings of South Western Pottery. The land was sold by the Receiver in June 1870 for £7,000 to John Kemp Welch of Clapham Common, Surrey, and, on his death, passed down to his five sons in equal undivided shares.

The eastern half of the Canford Cliffs Estate had had an equally complicated history; it was acquired in 1807 by an Edward Spencer, who borrowed £800 against it, offering the land as mortgage security. However, he never made any of the interest or capital repayments, and it took an action in Chancery lasting many years before the descendants of John Hunt, who lent him the money, were awarded possession in 1828. They sold the land in 1841 to Samuel Solly, a local landowner who had moved here from Lincolnshire and lived at Heathside on Evening Hill. On his death, it passed to his widow Dorothea, and then to their daughters.

Canford Cliffs

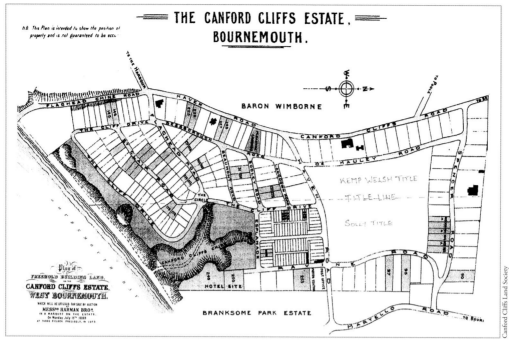

144. The plan from the first Auction of building plots in 1889, showing the only four houses built at that time. The 'title line' has been superimposed, showing the two areas of land which were combined to form the Canford Cliffs Estate.

Both halves of the site were purchased in 1885 by a Syndicate of five investors who had a far-sighted vision of a model village, laid out from scratch with shops, public open spaces, community facilities and building plots ranging in size from those for grand mansions to small semi-detached villas. Views of the sea from the clifftop, walks through the pinewoods, sandy beaches, accessible yachting facilities and the elegant shopping of Bournemouth within three miles, all combined in their view to make an irresistible residential location. Charles Robert Hutchings, Samuel Edward Kemp Welch and George James Piercy were solicitors, Reginald George Pinder was an architect and Thomas Bodley Scott a surgeon. Between them they raised the substantial capital necessary to pay the total purchase price of around £30,000,

145. A page from the Auction Particulars for a sale of building plots on the Canford Cliffs Estate in September 1898.

146. A postcard showing one of the first buildings to be completed in Haven Road, Canford Cliffs: the Post Office and tea rooms on the corner of Ravine Road. Haven Road crosses the picture, left to right.

Andrew Hawkes' Poole Picture Archive

147. A motor omnibus outside its office and waiting room in Canford Cliffs, from a photograph in the auction brochure from 1905.

Canford Cliffs Land Society

to lay out the road network incorporating sewers and water mains and to mark out the plots.

The first plots on the Canford Cliffs Estate were sold in 1886, when Cliff Drive was constructed and the road network was marked out eastward from Flaghead Chine as far as Spencer Road in the north and Ravine Road in the east. Initial sales of plots in the early years were encouraging, but purchasers were slow to build their houses. By the time Messrs Harman Brothers held the first public auction of plots in 1889, the site plan shows that dwellings had been constructed on only four of the 28 plots already sold. Further auctions were held in 1895 and 1898, by which time 14 houses and the first shop had been completed; by 1905 there were 30 houses and a large hotel, but it took 24 years to 1910 before the estate began to acquire a critical mass, with 75 houses, the hotel and seven shops.

The first shop to be built was the Post Office and tea rooms on the corner of Haven Road and Ravine Road and, by 1910 Grand Parade, the adjacent terrace was completed. The Syndicate had an interest in the Canford Cliffs Motor Omnibus Company which operated from premises further down Ravine Road. Roadways were marked out early on, from Flaghead Chine eastward to Ravine Road, and to Spencer Road in the north, including the Cliff Drive and The Esplanade, which were strong selling points for the estate.

Andrew Hawkes' Poole Picture Archive

148. Cliff Drive was one of the first roads to be constructed on the estate, because the sea views and bracing fresh air were one of its principal selling points. [9.7]

Andrew Hawkes' Poole Picture Archive

149. The Esplanade, with the public pleasure gardens and tennis court.

In view of the complicated history of the title to the land, the Syndicate took an early opportunity to register it at the Land Registry, to avoid the necessity of providing a lengthy Proof of Title for each plot. By 1900 they were able to offer 'Absolute Registered Title' and promise that 'Free Deeds of Conveyance will be Given', and in June 1907 the Syndicate itself takes on a more formal structure and is incorporated as The Canford Cliffs & District Land Company Limited. However, a slowdown in sales during the First World War and the recession which followed it, led in 1925 to the company being forced into liquidation, and its assets were transferred to Canford Cliffs Land Society Limited, which continues to administer the estate today.

The Canford Cliffs Estate was not without competition. By the time its plots were being offered for sale in 1886, most of the 750 acres of Branksome Park was marked out

150. The concrete house on the foreshore to the west of Flaghead Chine, built by John Simpson. This photograph was taken in 1880, in the brief period between its completion and its destruction by a storm, giving rise to its description as 'Simpson's Folly'.

for residential development. Building plots on Lord Alington's Lilliput Estate overlooking Poole Harbour had also been available since 1880, and in December 1879 the Poole and Bournemouth Herald carried an advertisement for 'Splendid Freehold Sites' for between two and twelve houses on the 'Poole Head Estate, only two miles and three-quarters from Bournemouth Pier'. This was a development by Lord Wimborne around the road today called 'Chaddesley Glen', although this was actually the name of one of the first houses to be built on the estate. Neighbouring Bournemouth also offered building sites for 'gentlemen's' marine residences' on the East and West Cliffs and at Westbourne. It was fortunate that this was a time when the British Empire was at its peak and wealth was being created by industry throughout the country. Examination of the Census Returns from the period show that a high percentage of the purchasers of new homes in Canford Cliffs, Lilliput and Branksome Park were successful businessmen who came from the Midlands and the North – a situation which is little changed today.

One of the most ambitious developments of this period was a building project which immortalised its promoter's name, but for all the wrong reasons. In 1878, a Mr John Simpson applied to Poole Council for permission to build several houses on the foreshore near Poole Head. Despite doubts expressed by several councillors as to the wisdom of building houses on sand, the plans were approved. In December of 1879 the first house was advertised as being ready within three weeks; entirely constructed of concrete, these were "*especially suitable for retired bathing and yachting boxes*" in which "*every care for their sanitary efficiency*" had been observed.

Alas for Mr Simpson, the worst forebodings of Poole's councillors were to be realised and the first of his massive concrete houses proved no match for the forces of nature. Within a few weeks of completion, a storm completely undermined the foundations and the house partly collapsed. The Council Engineer eventually had to dynamite the remains because they were judged a danger to the public. The resultant heap of concrete rubble remained on the foreshore for decades, known to Poole residents as 'Simpson's Folly'.

Canford Cliffs

It eventually proved to be useful hardcore in the construction of the promenade.

In about 1903 a purpose-built hotel opened its doors for the first time, situated in a prominent position at the end of Ravine Road, overlooking Canford Cliffs Chine and the Martello Tower on the cliff edge. The Canford Cliffs Hotel brought more people to the area, and advertised that it was "Patronised by Royalty", but was destroyed by an incendiary bomb in 1941; only the original stable block remains today, converted for use as a pub. St Ann's Hospital was completed in 1912, as a branch of the Holloway Sanatorium for the Insane in London.

As Canford Cliffs grew, the

151. Simpson's Folly after it suffered storm damage within weeks of completion. The Council's Engineer had to destroy it with dynamite because it was regarded as a danger to the public.

Poole Local Studies Centre

152. The Canford Cliffs Hotel, opened in 1903 overlooking the chine, with the Martello Tower on the cliff edge.

Andrew Hawkes' Poole Picture Archive

residents felt they should have their own church to avoid the necessity of travelling to the parish church, St Peters at Ashley Cross, or of using the closer, but rather less smart, Chapel of All Angels at Lilliput. In about 1908, the Rev. Hugh Pearson offered to donate an acre of land close to his house in Chaddesley Glen. There was much local debate as to whether this was too far out of the centre of Canford Cliffs Village, and the church council

153. St Anne's Hospital overlooking the sea at Canford Cliffs, completed in 1912.

154. The Church of the Transfiguration in Chaddesley Glen, soon after it was completed in 1911. It was designed as a temporary building with a timber frame and corrugated-iron roof, but lasted unchanged until 1964, when it was extended and reclad to create the beautiful church of today.

dithered for so long that a decision had not been reached by the time Hugh Pearson died. His Executors issued an ultimatum that, if the site were not accepted immediately, it would be put to auction in three weeks time, so a decision was eventually taken to put up a temporary building. The Church of the Transfiguration was completed in 1911, and there are many who still remember it today, because that "temporary" building lasted until the 1960s – indeed it has lasted to the present time, because the original structure is contained within the current elegant stone-clad building.

It seems surprising today, when Canford Cliffs is undoubtedly one of the most

Canford Cliffs

155. The shops in Haven Road, looking east, in the 1930s. Grand Parade, on the right of the picture, was the first terrace of shops to be completed in about 1910.

prosperous and well established residential areas in the borough – often referred to as the 'Diamond Ring District' – that two of the original companies promoting its development were forced into liquidation: both the West Bournemouth Land & Cliff Hotel Company in 1868 and the Canford Cliffs & District Land Company in 1925. As many of today's developers will undoubtedly testify, property speculation has always been a risky business!

Chapter 10

Industry at The Salterns

After a hundred years of manufacturing salt and another half century as a coal yard and industrial wharf serving the pottery, the area around the lagoon at Salterns was again called into use early in the First World War. It was still part of Canford Manor, and the transport links provided by the pier into the deep water of the harbour, and the railway line to Parkstone main-line station, gave it a strategic importance. New factory buildings were constructed and additional railway sidings laid down to equip the site as an engineering works. This was leased to Messrs W Alban Richards & Co. Ltd, a London-based company which undertook war-related work for the Government: making timber aircraft hangers for the Air Ministry and repairing railway rolling stock. A photograph of the site from about 1918 clearly shows how intensely it was being used for industrial purposes.

Britain was still at that time a leading shipbuilding nation and, towards the end of the War, it was clear that there an urgent national need to build more ships to replace the vessels lost in the hostilities, and to aid economic recovery. This resulted in two separate attempts to develop the salterns site as a major shipyard, both of which involved dredging the whole of the lagoon to create a huge commercial dock. Fortunately for Parkstone-on-Sea, both schemes failed; otherwise it might be a very different place today.

156. Salterns Works photographed from the harbour towards the end of World War I. On the left is a timber aircraft hangar under construction, before being disassembled and delivered to the RAF. Next to it appear to be railway wagons awaiting repair in the adjacent building and, on the right, South Western Pottery's old coal store building. On the hill above stands Salterns House which, it is clear, had a wide view over the harbour.

Poole Local Study Centre

Industry at The Salterns

Well before the end of the war, in 1917, when there was still a desperate national need for shipping, the Dorset Shipbuilding Company was first on the scene. Its promoters, headed by a Captain Gardener, were seeking a site on which it could build a major shipyard, which it envisaged would employ up to 10,000 men. The Minutes of Poole Harbour Commissioners record that several potential locations were considered, including one on the Purbeck shore near Arne, and another at Hamworthy; however, the eventual decision to settle on the Salterns site was dictated by its proximity to the main shipping channel, which reduced the amount of dredging needed. The scheme had the strong support of both the Commissioners and Poole Corporation, who wanted to expand maritime industry in the town, and because the promoters would have contributed cash to providing a solution to the Harbour Bar which had, for generations, limited the size of vessels able to enter the harbour.

The residents of Lilliput, Canford Cliffs and Sandbanks were appalled. They were relatively few in number, but felt that they should carry some weight in terms of money and influence. They submitted two 'memorials', letters signed by numerous householders, asking the Council to reconsider its support for the scheme. The first, from a group of residents in the districts of Salterns, Lilliput and Canford Cliffs assured the Council that while they were "*not lacking in any spirit of patriotism*", they all felt that "*the neighbourhood would be spoiled for residential purposes by putting shipbuilding on the site proposed, and they would be driven from their homes.*" A second memorial from another group, including Mr Colville-Hyde who had married the widowed Mrs Butts and now lived in Salterns House, "*begged to call attention to the fact that, while fully appreciating the importance of such an undertaking, they consider the site singularly unsuitable for such a purpose. The realisation of the scheme would damage a valuable residential neighbourhood, a health resort and an area of great attraction to visitors*", etc., etc.

These anguished pleas were debated at a meeting of Poole Council in January 1918, and the lengthy report in the East Dorset Herald highlighted the somewhat strained relationship between the hard-working tradesmen who made up the bulk of the Councillors and the residents of the Borough's prosperous outer wards. Councillor Woodford stated that "*he was sorry if the proposed scheme would interfere with the Canford Cliffs gentlemen, but they had piled up their money and even had their letters addressed 'Bournemouth'. They had stopped the trams and had poured cold water on every industry. Poole was a working class population and the Council should do everything possible to encourage that*".

Councillor Ayre agreed and said that "*he hoped no obstacles would be put in the way of the shipbuilding scheme. He had some experience of Sandbanks people: he did not want to charge them with not being patriotic, but they always put obstacles in the way of progress in Poole. They had used every power that they possessed, and cash, to prevent the trams going there...and to prevent people getting from Poole to Sandbanks*". All those who spoke in the debate were in favour of the shipbuilding scheme, and unanimously voted to send the memorialists the uncompromising reply that "*in the opinion of the Council, it is in the interests of the Borough that any proposal to establish industries should not be interfered with*".

Having obtained the backing of the Local Authorities and reached agreement with Lord Wimborne to buy the site, the promoters of the Dorset Shipbuilding Company set about obtaining the numerous other approvals necessary for a scheme of this magnitude.

These included the approval of the Treasury to go to the Stock Exchange to raise the £2,000,000 needed to carry out the development, the approval of the Board of Trade, the consent of the Controller of Auxiliary Shipbuilding and of The Shipbuilding Control Committee. The approval of the Admiralty Control Board was also essential to carry out the dredging necessary. The Company also needed guarantees under the Trades Facilities Act for any loans it took out.

This scheme failed. It was apparently thwarted by Members of Parliament for the north-country ship-building areas of the Clyde and the Tyne, who most certainly did not want a competitor in the South of England taking work away from their constituents. They are understood to have lobbied The Treasury to restrict the amount of capital that the Company was permitted to raise; this was duly limited to £500,000, making the ambitious scheme proposed by the Dorset Shipbuilding Company impossible to achieve. Its promoter, Captain Gardener, went on to develop a much smaller boatyard at Dorset Lake Shipyard at Hamworthy, which is still there today.

A second, more realistic, industrial development scheme emerged within a year, promoted in July 1918 by Messrs W Alban Richards & Co. Ltd, the engineering and woodworking company which leased the premises at Salterns from Lord Wimborne. The Richards family came from Ystrad in Wales and Alban and his brother Thomas were in business together in St James' Street, Mayfair, as Engineers and Building Contractors, constructing large estates of houses for local authorities, and manufacturing timber aircraft hangers for the newly-formed Royal Air Force and those civilians involved in the rapidly expanding pastime of flying small aircraft.

Alban Richards

157. An advertisement in the Times newspaper of May 1918 for Messrs W Alban Richards & Co. Ltd., the lessee of the industrial works at the salterns throughout the First World War. Aircraft hangers for the Royal Flying Corps., later the RAF, were manufactured in timber at the salterns.

No part of the proceeds of this Issue is to be applied for capital purposes outside the United Kingdom, or to replace money which has been so applied. The special permission of the Committee of the Stock Exchange required for dealing in these shares will be applied for together with an official quotation.

The Subscription List will open on the 29th day of October, and will close on or before the 4th day of November, 1919.

A copy of this prospectus has been filed with the Registrar of Joint Stock Companies.

SALTERNS LIMITED,
SHIPBUILDERS, REPAIRERS, ENGINEERS & TRANSPORTATION AGENTS,
POOLE HARBOUR, DORSET.
(Incorporated under the Companies Acts 1908 to 1917).

REGISTERED
152761
27 OCT 1919

SHARE CAPITAL - - £200,000
divided into
125,000, 7½% Cumulative Participating Preference Shares of £1 each.
75,000 Ordinary Shares of £1 each.

The Cumulative Participating Shares are preferential as to Capital and Dividend and in addition to receiving the preferential dividend of 7½% will be further entitled to 25% of the remaining profit which may be determined to be distributed in each year after the ordinary shares have received 7½%.

The Ordinary Shares receive 7½% of the profits after the 7½% has been paid on the Cumulative Participating Preference Shares as stated above and 50% of the remaining profits which may be determined to be distributed in each year.

The remaining 25% of the profits which may be determined to be distributed in each year will be transferred to trustees for the benefit and remuneration of the staff and employees of the company to be divided in such way and in such proportions as the deed of trust provides.

ISSUE OF £125,000

Being 75,000 7½% cumulative participating preference shares of £1 each at par, and 50,000 ordinary shares of £1 each at par payable as follows :—

				Preference Shares		Ordinary Shares	
On Application	..	..	..	2	6	2	6
On Allotment	..	..	..	2	6	2	6
December 1st, 1919	..	..	..	5	0	5	0
February 1, 1920	..	..	..	5	0	5	0
April 1st, 1920	..	..	..	5	0	5	0

Of the remaining shares 24,000 Preference Shares and 18,000 Ordinary Shares will be allotted as fully paid in satisfaction of the purchase consideration to the Vendors, as set out herein ; the balance of both classes of shares remaining will be held in reserve for future issue.

The National Provincial and Union Bank of England Ltd., Bishopsgate, London, E.C. 2. and Branches are authorised to receive subscriptions for the above issue.

DIRECTORS.
HENRY BURDEN, "Grantown," Wellington Road, Bournemouth, Shipowner.
J. E. EMLYN-JONES, "Kincoed," Roath Park, Cardiff,
(Managing Director Emlyn-Jones and Co., Ltd., Cardiff), Shipowner.
ALFRED JONES, "Pen-y-lan," The Avenue, Branksome Park,
(lately Director and Manager Hazlewood Shipping Co., Ltd., & Hopkins, Jones & Co., Ltd.,
Ship Owners and Brokers).
W. ALBAN RICHARDS, 53 South Audley Street, London, Contractor.
(Managing Director, W. Alban Richards & Co. Ltd.)
F. VAN RAALTE, Brownsea Castle, Poole Harbour (Director, W. Alban Richards & Co., Ltd.)
LT.-COL. H. W. WOODALL, C.I.E., M.INST. C.E., The Manor House,
Lytchett (Director Woodall, Duckham & Co.)
H. WRAGG, "Bretby," Near Burton-on-Trent (a Managing Director of Thomas Wragg
& Sons, Ltd., Swadlincote and South Western Potteries, Parkstone).

BANKERS:
THE NATIONAL PROVINCIAL AND UNION BANK OF ENGLAND, LTD., Parkstone.
SOLICITORS:
DICKINSON, YEATMAN & MANSER, POOLE, Solicitors for the Company.
COLLYER-BRISTOW & CO., 4, Bedford Row, London, W.C, Solicitors for the Vendor,
W. Alban Richards & Co., Ltd.
BROKERS:
ROBERT ESCOMBE, CAMPBELL & Co., 3, Crown Court, Old Broad Street, London,
and Stock Exchange.
AUDITORS:
WHEATLEY, PEARCE & CO., Poole.
T. ARNOLD EVANS & Co., 28, Threadneedle St., London, E.C.
FINANCIAL AGENT IN LONDON:
G. R. HOLMES, 27, & 31, St. Mary Axe, London, E.C., and Baltic Exchange.
SECRETARY & REGISTERED OFFICES:
(Lately of Admiralty Audit Staff), Salterns Works -Parkstone.

ATHERTONS
LIMITED,
COMPANY REGISTRATION AGENT

Andrew Hawkes' Poole Picture Archive

158. The front page of the Prospectus for the new company, Salterns Ltd., the main objective of which was to create a ship-building and repair yard at Salterns. Shares were offered on the Stock Market in October 1919, backed by a very impressive list of Directors.

himself was obviously an entrepreneur of considerable energy and, probably realising that the scheme by the Dorset Shipbuilding Co. failed because it was too ambitious, he nevertheless saw the potential for transforming the disused salterns into a major shipbuilding and repairing facility. The war was still raging, with no end in sight, and the need for more shipping was still just as vital.

Alban Richards first agreed a price of £36,000 with Lord Wimborne for the purchase of the freehold of the 62 acres of land and buildings which he leased from Canford Manor, which included the *"vendor's interest in the railway lines as laid to the said works, including the running rights over the private lines and sidings of Thos. Wragg & Co."*, together with a further 53 acres of "mudlands or foreshore" to include Salterns pier. He then formed a new company, Salterns Ltd, the prospectus for which is held in The National Archives, having been transferred from Companies House. He recruited what was described in the local paper as a *"strong Board of Directors, whose names are not only well-known in Dorset and Hampshire, but throughout the industrial world"*, ensuring that *"both the technical and general management is in capable and experienced hands"*.

These Directors included Henry Burden, a Harbour Commissioner and well-respected wharfinger and ship-owner in Poole, who was contributing to the new company the goodwill, plant and machinery of his West Shore Wharf in Poole; Florence Van Raalte, the aristocratic owner of Brownsea Island; Lieut-Col. H. W. Woodall, a civil engineer and director of Woodall, Duckam & Co., substantial local brewers; and Mr N Wragg, the Managing Director of South Western Pottery, over whose land the railway access ran. There were also two successful ship-owners, Mr Alfred Jones of The Avenue, Branksome Park, formerly director and manager of Hazlewood Shipping Company, the Green Star Shipping Company and of Messrs Hopkins Jones & Co.; and Mr J. E Emlyn-Jones, a ship-owner from Cardiff. These were all substantial and reputable people, each of whom injected a large amount of capital, or premises and goodwill, into the new venture.

The prospectus explains clearly the new company's objectives: these were:-
"to establish on Poole Harbour a shipyard, ship repairing base and engineering works; to purchase, develop and extend the marine and inland transportation business of Henry Burden & Co in Poole; and to purchase and develop the general engineering and woodworking business of W Alban Richards & Co Ltd".

The Directors make optimistic predictions as to the level of trade they expect the new business to generate which, in view of the experience of those running it, do not seem unrealistic. One interesting feature is the provision of a generous staff profit-sharing scheme. They state that *"in view of the labour unrest which is prevalent practically throughout the world, it is desirable and necessary in order to secure satisfactory labour relations to give those employed a direct stake in the success of the undertaking."* Quite a far-sighted approach.

Although not envisaging the employment of as many as 10,000 men, this second scheme to extend the already-substantial industrial development of the salterns would still have had a massive impact on the surrounding area. The railway line to Parkstone Station was already in place, having been built by the pottery some 40 years earlier, but the new company now had permission from the Harbour Commissioners to extend the line across the mudflats to Poole Station, so completely cutting off Parkstone Bay and Parkstone Yacht Club, in the same way that Poole Park lake had been cut off by the main line railway embankment in the early 1870s. The west side of the pier was to be reinforced to form 700 feet of substantial new commercial wharf, slipways were to be built running down into the harbour; and a new locked dock of about an acre excavated for smaller vessels. The lagoon itself, together with its approaches, was to be dredged to a depth of 15 feet at low water spring tides, and massive quay walls were to be built on three sides of it. All the proposed works had been costed in the Prospectus at a total of £90,000.

Industry at The Salterns

159. Salterns Works in 1918. The camera is by the Sandbanks Road, where the Lilliput shops are today; the lagoon is on the right, the pier is straight ahead and Jennings' coal-store building is on the left. The 'George Jennings' railway engine can be seen pulling several wagons, and more wagons are visible in the background on the right.

The new company, Salterns Ltd., was floated on the Stock Market in October 1919, with the object of raising £125,000. It wasn't completely successful, but shareholders subscribed almost £105,000, which was still sufficient to carry out the development works. But, within three and a half years, Salterns Ltd was put into Receivership. Despite owning excellent premises, having an established ongoing business, despite having experienced local directors and what seems to be adequate capital, it failed. And many years of research has still not revealed exactly why.

Certainly one problem was that of overcoming the bureaucracy of numerous Government departments. Although the proposed scheme was not as ambitious as that of the Dorset Shipbuilding Company, it still required numerous consents. Some of these undoubtedly were successfully obtained but, as late as January 1922, there is a Poole Council minute resolving to support Salterns Ltd in *"their application under the Trade Facilities Act 1921 for assistance in completing their scheme of wharfage, docks and ship repairing facilities in connection with their Salterns Works"*. Whether or not all the necessary consents were eventually forthcoming has not yet been established; unfortunately the file on Salterns Ltd from Companies House, now in The National Archives, relates only to the details of the flotation, and contains no subsequent corporate Minutes.

However, another possible reason for the company's failure is suggested by a descendant of one of the Directors of W Alban Richards & Co Ltd, researching her own family history, who has added more details to this story. Not only was Mr Alban Richards personally the main moving force behind the new company, Salterns Ltd, but his principal company, W Alban Richards & Co Ltd., was the largest shareholder and, in effect, its parent company. It seems that this business had expanded fast after the war, and by 1920 was running out

160. Part of the continuing business inherited by Salterns Ltd from Alban Richards & Co was repairing railway rolling stock, and this contemporary photo is taken inside the Wagon Repair Shed by the lagoon.

of working capital. At a meeting of the Preference Shareholders reported in The Times in April that year, the Board sought authority to alter the Articles of Association *"to enable the company to secure temporary loans or overdrafts from its bankers or others"*. The Chairman listed several local Authorities for whom they had major house-building contracts, and explained that they were daily turning down further work because they did not have the capital to fund it. He also reassured the meeting that the reason that the Preference Share price was so low was that the Underwriters had been left with unsold shares at the time of their issue the previous October, and had then disposed of their holdings at prices which the Board felt *"in no way reflects their intrinsic value"*. Shareholders were urged *"not to part with their shares at that price or anything like it"*. Those familiar with such matters will probably recognise the signs of a company under financial stress!

Family legend recounts that, soon afterwards, Alban Richards accompanied the Prime Minister, Lloyd George, on a business-seeking visit to the United States and initially found an investor prepared to inject more cash into the UK companies. However the deal went sour, the cash was never forthcoming and litigation resulted.

Alban Richards also had a falling-out with Mrs van Raalte, the wealthy owner of Brownsea Island in Poole Harbour, who was a director and large shareholder in both Salterns Ltd and W Alban Richards & Co Ltd. Whether she and the American investor referred to earlier are in any way connected, is not known, but various Notices in The Times do make it clear that the latter company was in serious difficulty. It seems that the Debenture Holders appointed a Receiver in 1923 and on 29th December of that year he advertised an Auction Sale in Bristol of *"substantial quantities of plant, machinery, building materials and vehicles"* belonging to the W Alban Richards & Co. On 29th January 1924, The Times reported on the compulsory, but unopposed, winding up of W Alban Richards

Labels on image: Sandbanks Road · Railway to South Western Railway · Lilliput · Elms Estate · Dock · Railway · Factory buildings · Parkstone Y.C. · Dock · Slipway · Approved rail extension to central Poole · To be dredged to 15 ft below LWS · 700 ft wharf

Andrew Hawkes' Poole Picture Archive

160. The extent of the development intended by Salterns Ltd, as shown in that company's Prospectus, is superimposed on a modern aerial photograph to illustrate just how much land (and harbour) would have been affected, had the company been successful. This was prepared by the Author for an article in Dorset Life magazine in October 2009.

& Co Ltd., and The Times Law Notices in July that year under the heading *"Companies (winding up)"* refer to a hearing in Chancery relating to *"W Alban Richards & Co Ltd (Van Raalte –v- W Alban Richards & Co Ltd)"*. Three more hearings of the same matter continue through to 1925.

Apparently the Director of W Alban Richards & Co Ltd whose descendant carried out this research had been warned by a colleague that the writing was on the wall for the company, but refused to believe it. When it did fail, he was personally bankrupted and took his own life in his grand house in Park Crescent, near Regents Park. It is said that he shot himself on the stairs to the staff quarters in the basement, so that the butler would hear and find his body, but not the members of his family asleep upstairs. His wife was left virtually penniless and had to move to a small flat with a single aged maid.

The financial problems of Mr Alban Richards, who had been the driving force behind the creation of Salterns Ltd, undoubtedly contributed to the collapse of both companies. In July 1923 a Receiver to Salterns Ltd was appointed by the High Court who, over the next couple of years, sold off all the company's assets. Exactly who purchased what is not entirely clear. There was certainly an attempt by a consortium of local residents to buy the lagoon itself, to prevent any further attempts at commercial development, but this may not have been successful because it was part of the freehold ownership of the Blue Lagoon Club when it opened in 1934.

The main site, extending from the eastern edge of the lagoon for the full length of Dorset Lake Avenue, was purchased by a consortium of investors headed by Henry Burden and Alfred Jones, both Salterns' directors, and Henry's brother, Augustus George Burden.

They resold part of it for £13,000 in July 1928, although they had to refer to the High Court for specific performance of the contract because Charles Michaux, the contracted purchaser, was prevaricating over completing the purchase, using the excuse that it was possible the railway lines to Parkstone Station might be removed – evidence that the rails were still in place at that time. Michaux sold it on again, because by the early 1930s, the land was owned the Bournemouth estate agent, George John Lattimer, who carried out the residential development of the Salterns Estate.

The one piece of commercial development which had already been completed by Salterns Ltd was the construction of a small dock on the east side of the main pier – the Minutes of both Poole Council and the Harbour Commissioners refer to the application early in 1922. This dock is now the inner basin of Salterns Marina, and its construction involved the moving of the sluice gates; these maintained the water level in the lagoon and were originally sited within the causeway at the approach to the pier built by George Jennings in 1867. They were moved to a new location in the breakwater, close to the Elms Estate, where their ruins can still be seen today, to the west of the current bomb-crater entrance to the lagoon.

If Salterns Ltd had not failed, the view from the Sandbanks Road today would be very different. In the middle of the lagoon would be a substantial deep water dock surrounded by concrete hardstanding, and the pier would be a massive wharf. This was illustrated for an article by the Author in Dorset Life Magazine, by superimposing the new company's design proposals from the prospectus onto a Google satellite image. The result gives some idea of the affect the development would have had on the Lilliput of today. This could well have been the catalyst to turn all of Parkstone-on-Sea into a massive industrial estate!

Industry at The Salterns

161. A rather grainy, but still recognisable photograph from the 1880s showing the view over Parkstone Village from Constitution Hill. In the centre is Charmouth Grove, in which many of these houses still remain today. It was the open countryside and elevated views towards the harbour which made the area so popular, both with affluent retired people and those who worked in Poole itself. Note that the construction of the new St Peter's church is not yet complete and the tower from the 1833 building is still standing.

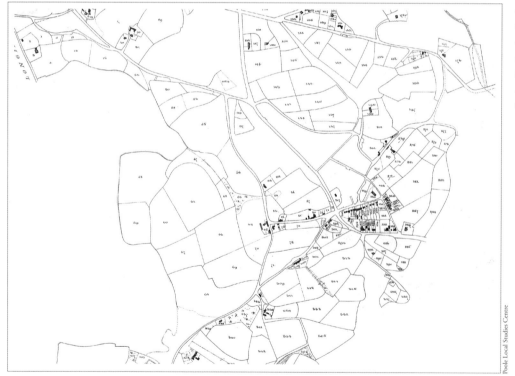

162. An extract from the Tithe Map of 1844 showing the extent of Parkstone Village at that time. Almost all development is in Parr Street and what was then Christchurch Road (now Commercial Road), with some extending down Britannia Road to Parkstone Farm at the junction with the Sandbanks Road. Parkstone Bay has not yet been cut in two by the railway embankment and extends almost up to the main road from Poole.

Chapter 11

Parkstone Village & Whitecliff

One of the main reasons for the growth of the outlying districts of Longfleet and Parkstone was that Poole Old Town was becoming an increasingly unpleasant place in which to live. Those who could afford it wanted to escape its squalor and overcrowding. Decades of bitter inter-party wrangling amongst Poole's very conservative councillors throughout the 19th century frustrated almost all improvements within the town. The Council refused to countenance the installation of an underground sewerage system until the end of the century, so night soil had to be collected from the streets and privies emptied by contractors. The inefficiency of the Poole Waterworks Company resulted in an irregular and inadequate water supply, and many of the public water pumps were contaminated by neighbouring cesspits. The Council also refused to finance an often-proposed system for washing down the streets with sea water. Infant mortality was disgracefully high, but the councillors would not believe that it had anything to do with the town's insanitary conditions. In fact, the town stank and those who were able to do so, moved to the countryside.

At the beginning of the 1800s, Parkstone Village was a modest hamlet a mile and a half outside the town, on the road to Christchurch. By the middle of the century it had become a thriving community with a church, school, Post Office, several pubs and a number of shops and other tradesmen to serve the growing population. Its wooded hillsides with views of the harbour, and pleasant surrounding countryside, started to attract residents from much further afield, and the 1851 census lists residents who have moved from Liverpool, Cornwall, Bristol, Essex, Norfolk and London. It describes a surprising number of these incomers as "of independent means", "annuitant", "fundholder", "gentleman" or as "land proprietor". There were numerous Royal Naval officers, some on half pay, together with other professions such as solicitors, physicians and clergy. Amongst the artisans with skilled trades were carpenters, bricklayers, blacksmiths, a hosier, shoemakers and shoe binders, cabinet makers, dressmakers, carters, gardeners and grooms. There were also numerous agricultural labourers and, as in any community at that time, a number of paupers.

The physical growth of the village can be traced through a series of maps, first the Ordnance Survey published in 1811, via the Parkstone Tithe Maps of 1841, 1844 and 1853 to the Ordnance Surveys of 1890 onwards. These show what is quite clear from walking the streets today, that the nucleus of residential development was originally around Ashley Cross and St. Peter's Church. One of the earliest photographs shows the church in the 1880s, still in course of being rebuilt, with cottages on one side of Parr Street only, but by the turn of the century both the new church and the street were complete. Shops and other

163. A very early photograph of Parkstone Village from about 1880. M[ ]Palmer's shop is whe[ ]the Central Hotel (now called The Ox[ ]stands today and we are looking up Parr Street to St Peter's Church which is stil[ ]in course of being rebuilt. The tower of the 1833 church is still standing.

St Peters Church from Church Rᵈ Parkstone.

164. A postcard from 1905 showing Church Road, now Parr Street, and the rebuilt St Peter's Church.

commercial premises sprang up on the main Christchurch Road (now Commercial Road). Larger villas and some quite substantial houses extended over the hillside to the north of the village centre, and up the hill on the main road towards Bournemouth. One of these, halfway up on the left, was The Castle, an early 19th century villa with crenellated towers at each corner, which gave its name to Castle Hill.

The land to the south of the village centre remained largely agricultural, with farms ranging in size from 10 to 150 acres. The biggest of these was Parkstone Farm, the buildings of which were located on the Sandbanks Road, opposite the junction with Britannia Road. In 1851 it is tenanted by George Foot, employing eight men, and in 1871 his land had

165. Commercial Road in Parkstone Village before the arrival of the trams. The recently-created park is on the left, at that time surrounded by iron railings.

166. The Castle, a substantial Victorian house which gave its name to Castle Hill which leads out of Parkstone Village towards Bournemouth. Post-war it was converted into flats and then pulled down in the 1960s.

Andrew Hawkes' Poole Picture Archive

167. A main road in Parkstone about 1900, with farm vehicles, illustrating how rural much of the area still was at that time.

Poole Local Studies Centre

been reduced to 90 acres, but he was now employing 21 labourers and 3 boys. His land was developed in the 1920s with Twemlow and Orchard Avenues.

Parkstone got a further boost in 1856 when George Jennings started to build his huge South Western Pottery. Although its kiln chimneys were not always the cleanest neighbour for those who lived close by, the pottery did provide a new source of employment in an area where the decline of maritime trade through the port and of the salt works had left agriculture as virtually the only source of work for the poorer classes. Of the 150 men employed by Jennings, some were undoubtedly in his London works, but the majority were in Parkstone.

A further encouragement to the development of what were known as the 'out-districts' came with the dissolution of Poole's Turnpike Trust. This was founded

by Act of Parliament in 1756 which empowered groups of local merchants and landowners to construct or improve the main roads in and out of the town, recovering costs by levying tolls on all road users except pedestrians and the stage coach. The first turnpike roads to be built in the 1760s were to Wimborne and to Ringwood, the latter going up Constitution Hill to Seaview, where the road to Christchurch branched off east along today's Ashley Road. Then, in 1810, increased traffic encouraged the construction of a turnpike in place of the lanes leading to Parkstone Village, offering a less severe incline up Castle Hill to the heath and distant Christchurch. In 1882 Poole Corporation took over the maintenance duties of the Trust and abolished tolls, which encouraged more people to move outside the town boundaries.

168. George Jennings' South Western Pottery from an advertisement of 1877. This provided significant employment in an otherwise largely rural area.

169. Parkstone Station in a postcard from 1905, when its signboard announced "PARKSTONE for SANDBANKS". Little had changed from its opening in 1874 or, indeed, to today!

Although it caused a major disturbance during construction, the arrival of the railway proved to be a great benefit in the long term. The embankment cut both Parkstone Village and Whitecliff in half, dividing the communities, but the opening of Parkstone Station in 1874 greatly improved communication for people whose only alternative means of travel was on foot or with a horse. At this time, there was limited employment in Poole itself, but the continued growth of neighbouring Bournemouth provided many jobs for Poole workers, which the railway made more easily accessible. The steady growth in the population also prompted the building of a bigger and better church: the original St Peter's, dating from 1833 in the Gothic style, was replaced piecemeal over some 15 years with the more impressive church of today, described at the time as "*a somewhat severe form of Early English design*". It was consecrated in parts between 1877 and 1901. However, the parish was never able to raise the funds to complete the planned tower and spire, which was originally intended for the northern end of the building.

St Peters Church (east end) Parkstone

170. Church Road, showing the rebuilt St Peters Church and a row of villas typical of those which attracted people to move out of the congested centre of Poole to a pleasant village environment.

171. A picnic in a farmer's field near Parkstone Village about 1905. Elegantly attired Edwardian ladies are providing tea for local children, most probably from St Peter's School. They are carefully segregated: the girls and other ladies are on the nearest table, with the boys at the one behind.

The growth in population of Parkstone Village was met with appropriate school facilities, first the Church of England elementary school of St Peters opened in 1833 in Church Road, at about the same time as the original church was consecrated. Then, in 1905, came Parkstone School, a private Church of England school in Commercial Road. This became Parkstone Girls Grammar School in 1937, and moved out of Ashley Cross to Fleetsbridge in 1958.

Also cut in two by the railway was Parkstone Bay. In the early part of the 19th century, the water of the bay extended much further inland, as far as today's Civic Buildings, and the road to Parkstone Village ran along its shore. Indeed, the pub on this road, The Sloop, is said to have been named after the ship which was regularly berthed close to it at the head of the bay. The construction of the railway embankment cut off what is today known as Poole Park Lake, although the boggy harbour shore had to be extensively reclaimed and landscaped to create the park itself. This was opened in January 1890 by HRH Edward, Prince of Wales, after a torrential rainstorm which destroyed all the Corporations lavish decorations.

By the latter part of the 19th century, Parkstone was marketing itself as *"England's Mentone"*. This means little to us today but, to the Victorians, the French Riviera was widely known for its blue seas and healthy climate and anybody who was anybody was to be seen holidaying there. A particular favourite was Menton, a few miles east of Monte Carlo, patronised by Queen Victoria in 1882, the first of many visits to the area. The official guide of the Parkstone Interests Association about the turn of the century states that *"Parkstone has been termed, and rightly designated, the 'Mentone of England' on account of its delightful position and equable climate"*.

In addition to Poole Park, the Council had also acquired a *"three acre field"* near Parkstone Railway Station as part of a land exchange with Lord Wimborne. This was

Andrew Hawkes/ Poole Picture Archive

172. On the left of this picture is the impressive facade of Ashley Cross School, a Church of England school privately founded in 1905 for boys and girls, which would later become Parkstone Girls Grammar School.

Poole Local Studies Centre

173. An aerial photograph from the late 1930s, with Poole Town in the foreground, Lilliput top right and Whitecliff and Parkstone Village top left. It clearly shows how much of Parkstone Bay was cut off by the railway embankment. Centre top is the first area of Whitecliff Recreation Ground to be reclaimed with household waste before the war. The 1960s reclamation which joined it to Baiter has not yet taken place.

174. Parkstone Park being enjoyed by local school children at the turn of the century.

View in Parkstone Park.

175. Ashley Cross, looking across Commercial Road to the new Parkstone Municipal Offices (now the Library), completed in 1899. This provided a large committee room, garaging for the fire engine, mess room for the firemen and stabling for four horses.

Poole Local Studies Centre

landscaped to create Parkstone Park and was opened by the Prince on the same day as Poole Park. Then in 1899 the district also got its own Municipal Offices. These housed a committee room, accommodation for a fire engine, stabling for four horses and a mess room for the firemen, and is now Parkstone Library. The number and variety of traders increased steadily over the years, and further local facilities came to the village in 1909 when five acres of land in Salterns Road were acquired from Lord Wimborne for the creation of what is still today the East Dorset Lawn Tennis and Croquet Club.

176. As Parkstone grew, so did the number and variety of traders serving the needs of the residents. Without refrigeration, milk and any perishable foods had to be obtained daily, and Parkstone Dairies advertised 'Deliveries twice daily'.

177. A party of Edwardian picnickers on the beach of Parkstone Bay, beneath the white cliffs which gave the district its name. Today, Whitecliff Road runs along the top of those cliffs.

What remained of Parkstone Bay after the loss of some 50 acres to Poole Park was further eroded by reclamation in the 1930s. Before that, the waters of the harbour came almost up to the Sandbanks Road and formed a beach under the cliffs beneath Whitecliff Road. Those cliffs, largely kept clear of vegetation by waves and weather, were a striking white – hence Whitecliff! They contained caves which were a playground for local young, and the beach was a favourite picnicking and swimming spot. Sandbanks Road and Turks Lane were regularly flooded by high tides and so Poole Council took the opportunity to

178. An aerial taken in the late 1930s showing the Park Estate and the keyhole bridge in the foreground, and the Elms Estate beyond. The flat area, now part of Whitecliff Recreation Ground, was reclaimed with household rubbish in the early 1930s. Before that, the waters of Parkstone Bay came almost up to the Sandbanks Road, and until the 1960s, right up to the cliff beneath Whitecliff Road.

Gordon Cousins

179. Commercial Road looking east towards Parkstone Park in about 1910, with a 'Bluebell' tram en route to Poole.

reclaim the shallowest area adjoining these roads by filling it with household refuse – many local residents still remember it as "the tip". More extensive reclamation was to take place in the 1960s to create Baiter and Whitecliff Recreation Ground.

The trams came to Poole in 1901. Poole & District Electric Traction Company proposed a route between Poole Station and County Gates which went through Parkstone Village, but the traders objected to the idea of the tramlines and overhead wires and so these

180. Commercial Road at Ashley Cross about 1910, looking west, with contrasting forms of transport.

PARKSTONE, FROM THE EMBANKMENT.

181. The southern part of Parkstone Village just before the First World War, with St. Peter's Church in the background. A lady pushing a perambulator is emerging from the arch under the railway on the Sandbanks Road, and Tennyson Road stretches out to her right. On the left is a Nonconformist Church and what remains of Parkstone Farm, reduced to a market garden.

were laid up North Road to Seaview and along Ashley Road instead. The new service proved immensely popular with the public and it was not long before the residents and tradesmen of Parkstone realised their mistake. It took seven years, but eventually a second line was laid from Park Gates East, along Commercial Road and Bournemouth Road to Pottery Junction at Branksome. Trams, however, had a relatively short life, and were replaced by the motor omnibus in 1929.

By the early years of the 20th century another part of Parkstone had grown into a thriving community. What had once been open heathland on the ridge running from Branksome Pottery to Seaview was now covered with cottages and small villas on either side of Ashley Road. This was known as 'Upper Parkstone' and, as a result, Parkstone Village and its surrounding area was increasingly referred to as 'Lower Parkstone', even if it did consider itself a cut above its largely artisan neighbour. The bus companies adopted these names on their destination boards, so their use became universal. As with other parts of the borough, residential development of all the open fields continued apace between the wars, although Parkstone Village itself changed relatively little. Indeed, this small area centred around the cross roads, with its Victorian terraces and villas and narrow lanes, remains the only part of the whole district which still today retains some of its original 19th century feel – the rest of Parkstone-on-Sea has changed beyond all recognition.

182. A postcard entitled 'Sandy Lane, Parkstone', sent soon after the Golf Club opened, illustrating how rural the surrounding area was at that time. This is today one of the longest, widest and straightest roads in the Borough - Canford Cliffs Road.

Chapter 12

The Golf Course

Today, as one drives down the steep hill on Lilliput Road, probably just a little too fast and concentrating on negotiating the sharp corner at the bottom, one is briefly aware of the green open space of the golf course stretching away on both sides of the road. However, it is not unless one has the privilege of being a member of Parkstone Golf Club that one fully appreciates what an extensive and beautiful open space it provides right in the heart of densely-developed suburban Parkstone.

We owe this important local asset to Lord Wimborne, on whose estate of Canford Manor it was constructed. His motives were not entirely altruistic: golf was an increasingly popular game in the later years of the Victorian and Edwardian eras and Lord Wimborne had already developed the Dorset Golf Club at Broadstone, because he knew it would increase the attraction of the neighbouring parts of his estate for residential development. He applied the same strategy to Parkstone, which was surrounded by open heathland known originally as 'Canford Launnes' and more recently as Poole Heath. Some forestry planting of pines had been carried out, but the growth of neighbouring Bournemouth and the residential development of Branksome Park, Canford Cliffs and Lilliput offered hope that the areas inland might also offer profitable opportunities for housing development.

Evidence that the strategy had a rapid affect comes from a guide to *"Parkstone; England's Mentone"* published by the 'Parkstone Interests Association' in 1914. Making allowances for the promotional hype and flowery language of the day, it is still clear that the heathland surrounding the golf links was undergoing a transformation: *"At the foot of Stromboli hill are the Golf Links, which have had a large share in the promotion of the surrounding district, and the many handsome houses and broad avenues that are arising amid the heather and the gorse, testify to its charms as a residential country, a place of rest and peace, 'far from the madding crowd'."*

Another factor was that most of the land on which the golf course is constructed is not suitable for building. It is the valley of the Luscombe stream, and some 23 acres had already been sold off in about 1890 to the Poole Water Company for the construction of the Parkstone Reservoirs which still form a feature of the course today. South of Lilliput Road lies the original Pumping House, beneath which were constructed two vast brick water-storage cisterns, capable of holding several million gallons, and these are understood still to be in place. There were also several cottages used by company staff. The water company had never been efficient at providing a reliable supply, nor was the water quality entirely satisfactory, and was eventually acquired by Poole Council in about 1906, and these

183. *A postcard sent in 1913 shows Parkstone Golf Course and Clubhouse soon after it opened in 1910, with the harbour, Sandbanks and the Purbeck Hills in the distance. At this time the fairways extended south only as far as the Lilliput Road.*

184. *A photograph of the golf links from a local guide published in 1914 which eulogises Parkstone as "England's Mentone" A lady is seen walkin along what is today Lilliput Road.*

Colin Stone

works were abandoned. Wishing to include them in his new golf course, Lord Wimborne negotiated an exchange with the Council, re-acquiring the waterworks land in exchange for The Ladies' Walking Field in Poole, on which the Dolphin Centre now stands.

Construction of Parkstone golf course started in June 1909 and was completed by some 300 workmen in only five months, although unsurprisingly it was not until May 1910 that it was deemed fit for play to commence. The clubhouse was sited at the northern edge of the course, at the end of St Osmond's Road, eschewing the better views further south for proximity to the tram routes and Parkstone station, in an era when few people had cars.

Lord Wimborne set up the original committee, with himself as President and his third son, the Hon. Freddie Guest as Chairman and Captain, together with five others. These then nominated the rest of the initial members - 100 men and 30 ladies. Their annual subscription was 2 guineas. The Wimborne's ownership of the Club continued for about twenty years, until the second Baron, Ivor Churchill Guest, who inherited in 1914 and was made a Viscount in 1918, moved his main seat to Ashby St Ledger, and started to dispose of any part of the Canford Estate which was not providing a good investment return. This included the Manor House, which was sold as a school in 1923, and then the golf course was offered for sale to the members in 1927 at £20,000. A consortium of six members (with the help of the owner of Compton Acres, who did not want his view spoiled by housing development) was able to raise the cash and it became Parkstone Golf Club Ltd.

The course was not then the size it is today. Originally it extended from the main entrance in Links Road only as far south as Lilliput Road. The land to the south of this belonged to the Sturt family of Moor Crichel, and was very boggy, drained by the Luscombe stream. Indeed, where Lilliput Road now crosses that stream is marked on the map from 1770 by Isaac Taylor (see Chapter 3) as *"the foord & passage where the wains pass"*; i.e. wagons could ford the stream at this point.

It was only in the 1930s that the Club acquired the land to the south of Lilliput Road, extending further down Luscombe Valley. This had always formed part of Flag Farm which, with the hills on either side of the valley, had been owned since the 18th century by the Crichel Estate. The Sturts, now ennobled as the Lords Alington, had been developing the higher land since the 1880s, selling off or leasing plots for residential development and the boggy valley with its stream was left over, being incapable of development.

Negotiations between the Club Secretary and Crichel's Agent opened in 1928 and proved both protracted and complicated, not only because the Golf Club needed to raise the money from a consortium of members, who frequently disagreed with each other, but also because Poole Corporation was considering designating the whole valley as public open space. Eventually a compromise was reached: in May 1932, Lord Alington sold 53 acres to Parkstone Golf Club Ltd for £5,000, and donated the bottom of the valley to the Corporation as a nature reserve, which is still the situation to this day.

Frank Henson

185. The dock built by Salterns Ltd in 1922, in use by Mr Knight who ran Woodside boat yard. This was later used by The Harbour Club, and then by Air Sea Rescue craft and BOAC's launches serving the flying boats. Today it is the Inner Basin of Salterns Marina.

Chapter 13

Parkstone Between the Wars

Although development got off to a slow start after the First World War ended, it was the inter-war period of the 1920s and 1930s which transformed the predominantly rural Parkstone-on-Sea into the popular residential district of Parkstone which is recognisable today. The farms and their green fields steadily disappeared under new houses; new roads were laid out to create residential estates and the main roads were gradually made up with pavements and metalled surfaces.

House-building in Parkstone increased in pace in the late 1920s, a major catalyst being the opening of the Sandbanks chain ferry in 1926. Ribbon development of houses took place all along the Sandbanks Road, and new estates were started on Elms and Pearce Avenues, Salterns Way and Dorset Lake Avenue, Sherwood Avenue and the Park Estate in Whitecliff, as well as off Compton Avenue by the golf course. By the early 1930s, many of the buildings we know today were taking shape. Parades of local shops were being built on the Sandbanks Road at Whitecliff and at Lilliput, and on Sandbanks in Banks Road.

After the failure of Salterns Ltd, the Receiver sold off that company's assets piecemeal. The industrial works and part of the land were bought by a consortium of speculators, including several of the Salterns directors, and in 1926 they contracted to resell the land to a local developer, Charles Michaux, who had already reclaimed areas of mudland at Sterte for building. His intentions seem to have been to extend and strengthen the pier as a shipping wharf and to build further factories, but the Harbour Commissioners would not consent to any further narrowing of the main shipping channel at this point, and apparently South Western Pottery and Lord Wimborne were considering the removal of the railway line to the pier, which was very little used. The vendors had to take legal action to require Michaux to complete the purchase at the agreed price of £13,000, and nothing became of his scheme.

For several years nothing happened to the land. A gypsy camp had become established on the site and, when eventually the smart new Salterns Residential Estate was planned, the gypsies were apparently removed in a fairly heavy-handed manner. As a result, there is a story that they put a curse on the land and all that were to live there. History suggests that this did not prove to be very effective, because this has always been an affluent and successful residential area. We do know that Mr J R H Knight ran Woodside Boatyard (which would later be known as Pizey's yard), at the eastern end of Dorset Lake Avenue, and he used the abandoned dock. This can be seen in photograph 185, with a notice saying

186. An advertisement by the timber merchants, Sherry & Haycock, in the 1930s showing their factory and storage sheds where Wedgewood Drive is today. Sandbanks Road runs across the bottom of the picture, with the Model Farm Dairy on the right and South Western Pottery and Pottery Road beyond.

"Please sound horn for attendance." Otherwise the Alban Richards factory buildings were left to decay and the railway lines were eventually taken up in about 1928.

However, industry was still interested in Parkstone, and in 1922, an old-established local firm of timber importers and merchants, Sherry & Haycock Ltd, purchased a large site on the Sandbanks Road from South Western Pottery for £1,305. On this they built an extensive, but unsightly, range of timber storage and woodworking buildings with corrugated iron roofing which they continued to occupy until 1972. It was then redeveloped as the Wedgewood Drive Estate.

Parkstone Yacht Club had survived the war with very little disruption, so it was a shock in 1918 when it became known that proposals had been approved by Poole Council and the Harbour Commissioners to build a massive shipbuilding yard at Salterns (see Chapter 10), and the Committee commissioned a professional valuation of their own premises, assessed at £1,200. Fortunately the shipyard plans never materialised. After that, the club took every opportunity to extend its site, and in 1924 purchased from the Harbour Commissioners the mudlands extending out to Westons Island for £25. The following year, at the start of the development of the Elms Estate, it bought the building site adjoining the yard entrance, which cost £400 for a quarter acre, with the intention of eventually erecting a new clubhouse. However, the first priority was a boatshed, which was completed in 1926, and the clubhouse followed by 1931; it was designed as a chalet bungalow to give the option

187. The new clubhouse for Parkstone Sailing Club, completed in 1931. As is often the case in clubs, there were strong disagreements amongst members about such an extravagant project, so it was built in a form which could be sold off as a private house, if the club fell on hard times. It still forms the core of today's clubhouse.

188. The first parade of shops on the Sandbanks Road at Lilliput, built by John Jagger in about 1930. Jagger's yard and bungalow lie behind the shops, and his signboard can just be seen on the extreme left of this picture.

THE SQUARE, LILLIPUT.

189. Salterns Court on the Sandbanks Road at Lilliput, built by Whitelocks in 1937. On the right of this picture is a shop occupied today by Oddbins, which from 1937 – 1941 was run by Fred Karno, the one-time music hall impresario.

of selling it off if the club fell on hard times. Although it has had many alterations and additions, this still forms the core of today's clubhouse.

It was not until the early 1930s that what we now regard as the centre of Lilliput started to develop. A local builder, John Jagger, who had bought part of the Salterns site from the Receiver, built a bungalow for himself in Salterns Way, on the corner of what is now Lagoon Road, with his yard next door. He then developed the Sandbanks Road frontage of this site with the first parade of Lilliput's shops, those which today house Tesco Express. This was followed in 1937 by the shops and flats of Salterns Court, built by Whitelock & Co., a local building firm founded in 1899 and still going strong today in the hands of the fourth generation of the family.

In May 1932, the new Municipal Buildings were opened at Park Gates East, on the western edge of Whitecliff. The Council had bought the 3.75 acre site in 1923 for £4,400, and the building was designed by the Borough Engineer, Ernest Goodacre on what were

described as 'restrained neo-classical' lines. This was also built by Whitelocks, and the total budget was £62,500.

In April 1933, the Minutes of Poole Council record the granting of planning consent for a new "Club house and tea room" on the Sandbanks Road, close to the Elms Estate, and backing on to the old salterns. Its owner, a Mr P. Kimberley, gave his new club the somewhat exotic name of "The Blue Lagoon", and that name has stuck ever since, despite the inescapably murky hue of the lagoon's water!

Mr Kimberley's new club provided a bar, a large ballroom, dining and changing facilities. Outside was a 75 ft. swimming pool, parking for 50 cars and a petrol pump. The lagoon became a 40 acre boating lake with fleet of sailing dinghies, rowing boats and punts. An attendant, elegantly attired in blazer and white flannels, supervised the pool and the dinghies sailing on the lagoon which, like Poole Park lake today, was kept at a constant depth of between three and four feet by sluice gates in the outer breakwater. The original club building and pool have since been redeveloped, but many local people remember learning to swim or sail dinghies here. A local lady, today a sprightly 97 years young, recalls

193. *The water in the lagoon was kept at a constant depth by sluice gates in the outer breakwater, which can just be seen on the extreme right of this picture. This enabled a fleet of sailing dinghies, punts and rowing boats to be used by club members .*

194. *Advertisement from the Poole Town Guide in 1939, showing the Harbour Club soon after its completion in 1934. Note that the bar extension in front of the squash court was not added until some years after the club was opened.*

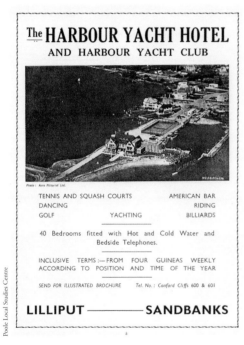

winning her race in the Swimming Gala at the opening of the club in 1934.

Later that same year, a second new club opened on the edge of the lagoon - a yacht club in Salterns Way. This was a rather more ambitious enterprise. Now known as the Salterns Hotel, many will remember it as the Poole Harbour Yacht Club; but it opened in July 1934 as The Harbour Yacht Hotel, advertised with the catch-phrase: a *"West End club by the sea"*.

The smart new mock-Tudor premises were built on part of the site which had been occupied by the failed industrial company, Salterns Ltd, just after the First World War. It was financed entirely on borrowed money by Richard Preston, aged only 26, one of two sons of a local hotelier, Madge Preston, who owned the Seaview Hotel in Ashley Road and probably stood as guarantor of the loan from the County of London Building Society.

Preston had previously leased and run the Harbour Quay Club in Poole, which he sold as a going concern for £1,500. Then, early in 1933, he purchased 12 acres of land at Salterns, seven acres of which was under water, at a price of £3,300. Construction was not cheap: in addition to a high quality main building costing £7,700, which is still there today in the form of Salterns Hotel, he spent another £2,500 on furnishings, a cash register,

Woodford Family

195. Dickie Preston
(with champagne)
with family and
friends at the
opening of The
Harbour Club in
1934.

Poole Local Studies Centre

196. The Harbour
Club soon after
it was opened in
1934, before the
addition of the
bar extension on
the right of the
elevation facing
the harbour. The
lagoon is in the
foreground.

electrical fittings and a petrol pump. Much of the site had to be reclaimed and landscaped at a cost of £3,271 to accommodate the full-sized squash court, tennis court and to smarten up Jennings old pier for launching dinghies. The dock which had been constructed by Salterns Ltd in 1922, provided sheltered berthing for members' boats, but the entrance channel had to be dredged again after years of neglect.

The Harbour Club opened its doors on July 21st 1934. The annual subscription was two guineas and, over the next couple of years, it recruited about a thousand members.

According to family legend, both Dickie Preston and his wife, Theresa, enjoyed the high life, and were somewhat cavalier about such things as observing licensing hours and keeping proper accounts. Within a year the local paper carried a report of a police raid on an after-hours drinking party, doubtless tipped off by exasperated residents in their new houses in Salterns Way, who had frequently complained of disturbance from club members leaving late at night.

By early 1936 Preston, now aged 28, was bankrupt and The Poole & East Dorset Herald reports in May on his examination before the Bournemouth Bankruptcy Court, which revealed he had accumulated debts of over £8,000. His mother had to bail him out by buying the club and paying off what had, by then, risen to four mortgages! Dickie Preston joined the Navy at the beginning of the war and, after he was demobbed, ran the White Hermitage Hotel in Bournemouth.

Although Madge Preston did run The Harbour Club for a short time after she had bailed out her son, she then sold it on; exactly who owned it for the next few years is not absolutely clear. The Street Directory for 1939 cites the Proprietors as Cmdr. P.L. and Mrs Frampton, and the edition of 1940 lists Mr C A McArdle as Managing Director of The Harbour Yacht Club Ltd. It is in the latter's name that a planning application is made in July 1938 for the three-storey Bar and Bridge Room extension, which filled in the gap next to the squash court. What is certain is that whoever did incur the considerable cost of extending the clubhouse at this time was most unlucky – within a few months they would lose the use of it for almost 10 years, requisitioned by the Government in connection with the coming war!

197. A postcard sent during the war showing the Harbour Club with the addition of the 1939 extension to provide a bar and card room above. In the centre of the picture are the new marine villas of the Salterns Estate, with the Lilliput shops beyond.

The building of the Harbour Club in 1934 was the catalyst for the development of the Salterns residential estate and the construction of the houses in Salterns Way, Dorset Lake Avenue and the adjoining roads. By this time, the owner and developer of the land appears to have been a Bournemouth Estate Agent, George Lattimer. He advertised his houses in, amongst other publications, the Poole Guide, and the one thing that has not changed in three-quarters of a century is the advertising blurb used by estate agents: the Salterns Estate is described, somewhat optimistically, as "adjoining Sandbanks"!

It took until 1939 for all the plots in Salterns Way to be sold and developed. A few of those original houses remain, both in the Art Deco 'marine villa' style and as almost rustic cottages, one of which is believed to have been judged 'House of the Year' at the Ideal Home Show at Olympia. However many have been torn down and replaced with massive modern houses, or two houses on one original site.

Several new hotels also sprang up around the harbour shore and the beaches of Poole Bay. As explained in an earlier chapter, the Haven Hotel had been established since 1880 on North Haven Point, but its original Victorian villa had grown in stages to become a substantial hotel by the late 1930s. It remains today a popular hotel in a commanding position at the entrance to the harbour, with fine views over the Purbeck Hills.

198. An aerial view of Lilliput and the Salterns Estate taken in about 1937. Salterns Way and the Harbour Club dock are in the centre, with Dorset Lake Avenue and Gardens Crescent in the foreground. . The scars where the pottery railway lines have been removed can be seen along the edge of the lagoon, and there are now three blocks of shops on the Sandbanks Road.

199. The Haven
Hotel on North
Haven Point, taken
in 1938. The Ferry
Cafe is to its left.

Similarly, the Sandbanks Hotel had grown from Sir Ernest Cassel's seaside villa, Sand Acres, to become a very successful family hotel fronting directly onto the beach. Nearby, the Sandacres Hotel was completed in 1936 in a very typical Art Deco style of architecture, but this business did not stand the test of time and the building was converted into 17 flats in 1962, with just a bar on the ground floor remaining open to the public. That has now become a Tesco Express.

The Harbour Heights Hotel was constructed originally just after 1900 as an Edwardian-style detached house called 'East Looe'. It was then extensively remodelled as a hotel in the early 1930s by the Architects, A J Seal & Partners, in an Art Deco style, and the adjacent Conning Tower built in keeping. They were described by Nikolas Pevsner as 'a brave and enterprising group of early modern buildings, admirably sited, with prominent glazed staircase curves derived from Mendelssohn.'

After the First World War, Jennings' Model Farm had been acquired by Froude's Dairies, who also had substantial premises in The Triangle in Bournemouth. The milk rounds in Parkstone were made by smart delivery carts with rubber tyres, drawn by high-stepping trotting horses. However in August 1936, the dairy was at the centre of a major typhoid epidemic which affected more than 700 residents and visitors who had consumed

200. A postcard of the Sandbanks Hotel from about 1937. The gable of the original Victorian house, "Sand Acres", can still be distinguished towards the right hand end of the building.

201. The Sandacres Hotel on Banks Road, soon after completion in 1936. It stood on the site of the staff cottage for Sand Acres.

Poole Local Studies Centre

202. A postcard showing The Harbour Heights Hotel in Haven Road in the mid 1930s, which enjoyed magnificent views over the harbour and Poole Bay. To its right is The Conning Tower, a block of flats in a matching Art Deco style.

203. This 1937 aerial shows the Harbour Heights Estate on the left and the Poole Head or Chaddesley Estate on the right, with Shore Road and 'The Hive' in the foreground. The original route of Haven Road, which continued in a straight line down Haven Hill to the harbour edge, is readily distinguishable. This proved too steep for horse-drawn traffic, resulting in the construction of West Road which takes a more gentle gradient to the left of the picture.

Poole Local Studies Centre

its milk, causing 51 deaths. Many of those who did survive, but in the process had become carriers themselves, were not released from isolation hospital for more than a year.

The dairy itself, its equipment and its hygiene, was found to be blameless. Poole's Medical Officer, Dr Vernon Shaw, traced the source to a farm at Merley, near Wimborne, which supplied the dairy with unpasteurised milk, where a stream had been contaminated by a leaking drain from Merley House. On testing the residents, it was found that the

204. A typical milk cart, such as those used throughout the first half of the 20th century in Parkstone and rural areas all over the country.

Andrew Hawkes' Poole Picture Archive

Andrew Hawkes' Poole Picture Archive

205. A photograph used by Froude's Dairy in an advertisement of 1927, emphasising the purity of its milk. Ironically this was only a few years before the company was put out of business by the typhoid epidemic caused by milk that it supplied.

Gordon Cousins

206. The Elms Estate in course of development in the mid 1930s, with Parkstone Yacht Club's piers to the right of the picture, and the Harbour Club on the other side of the lagoon.

owner, Captain Angus Hambro, from 1910–1922 MP for South Dorset, was a carrier of the bacillus, having travelled extensively in the tropics. Despite being blameless, Froude's business collapsed and the company was bought out by its main competitor in Bournemouth, Malmesbury & Parson, who continued to use the Model Farm until it was redeveloped as part of the Wedgewood Drive Estate in the 1970s.

Development of the Elms Estate had started slightly earlier than on Salterns Estate. The land was still owned by Daniel Sunderland, the great-nephew of William Pearce, and planning consent was granted by Poole Corporation in August 1922 to build the roads

207. An aerial picture of Parkstone taken in about 1937. Parkstone mainline station is in the foreground, with South Western Pottery in the centre and Sherry & Haycock's timber yard on the right. Beyond them lies the Harbour Club and Blue Lagoon, with Sandbanks and Studland in the distance.

Mary Cooper

and sewers. However it was not until 1925 that Sunderland started to offer the plots for sale, and it seems that construction of the roadways of Elms and Pearce Avenues were not actually completed until about 1927. Houses were built gradually over the next 12 years, but completion of the estate would not happen until after the imminent war.

Aerial photos of the area in the late 1930s show how much undeveloped land still remained. Sandbanks is only partly developed; open fields in Lilliput still grazed residents' ponies, and the timber merchants, Sherry & Haycock, remain in occupation of a massive range of unsightly industrial buildings on the Sandbanks Road. South Western Pottery was still in active production and, although some of its original land had been sold off for residential development, it remained a major industrial presence in the heart of Parkstone.

Parkstone Between the Wars

208. A Shorts C Class flying boat taking off. These were the first boats to arrive in Poole, having been developed in 1936 as the result of a Government contract with Imperial Airways to transport mail and freight to all parts of the British Empire.

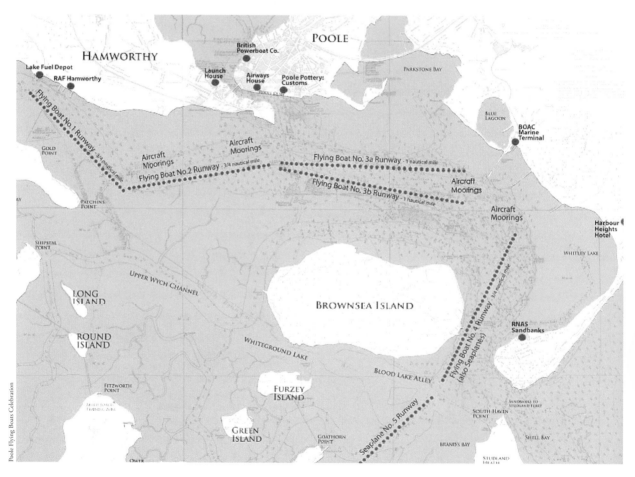

209. This map was prepared by Poole Flying Boats Celebration to show the runways laid out in Poole Harbour for the flying boats and seaplanes during the Second World War, together with the location of their moorings. The principal land-based facilities are also marked.

Chapter 14

The Flying Boat Era

The building boom of the 1930s was stopped in its tracks, of course, when war was declared in September 1939. However, this was the start of what was, perhaps, to be Parkstone's finest hour, when Poole Harbour became Britain's principal international airport and the massive flying boats kept open our war-time communications with the farthest parts of the Empire and North America.

After the First World War, seaplanes and flying boats, with their flexibility to land wherever there was sheltered water, were seen as the future of air transport. Their profile had been raised in the September of 1919 by the Schneider Trophy Contest, a race for seaplanes carried out round Poole Bay, following which several British manufacturers developed larger passenger-carrying machines. A major impetus came in 1934 when the Government announced that, to link the many scattered countries of the British Empire more closely, it intended that all overseas mail should go by air, at the same price as internal mail within Great Britain.

The Empire Air Mail Scheme resulted in greatly increased volumes of overseas mail, in response to which Imperial Airways, with Government backing, commissioned a new generation of flying boats from the leading manufacturer, Short Brothers of Rochester. These were large four-engined craft, capable of carrying 24 passengers in considerable comfort, together with one and a half tons of freight. They had a range of 800 miles and a speed of 150 miles an hour. Initially designated the S-23, they became to be known as the 'Empire' boats from their intended destinations, or the 'C-Class', because all 28 were given names starting with the letter C. Indeed, names were an integral part of the mystique of flying boats, which were always referred to by all those who worked with them as 'boats', rather than 'aircraft' and, as such, names were an important means of identification.

In 1937 Imperial Airways established a base at Southampton for the operation of its new fleet of Empire class flying-boats, basing its maintenance workshops at Hythe and landing its passengers on the opposite side of Southampton Water, close to Royal Pier. However, two years later, with war looming, the area was becoming increasingly busy with shipping and it was anticipated that it would be a prime target for enemy bombers, so alternative arrangements soon had to be made. Although smaller, the sheltered waters of Poole Harbour, only some 30 miles to the west, were seen as a workable alternative. At the time of the Munich Crisis in 1938, the RAF carried out a survey of Poole Harbour and contingency plans were drawn up to move Imperial Airways' flying boat operations there in the event of war.

210. Airways House, No.4 High Street, Poole (now the Museum) which was the headquarters of BOAC's flying boat operations from 1939 – 1948.

At the outset of war, the harbour was cleared of all private craft, and heavyweight moorings were laid off Salterns Pier for the civilian flying boats. Although the War Department had initially requisitioned the Harbour Club for use by the Army, Salterns pier was designated as a RAF facility, and it was the RAF that marked out marine runways for the flying boats. These were broadly in the positions shown on the accompanying chart prepared by Poole Flying Boats Celebration. The use of these runways depended very much on wind direction and the state of the tide – at low water, some were unusable, although the sheltered nature of the harbour meant that there was almost always one accessible runway. In the dark, they had to be marked by small dinghies containing a lantern, and keeping these in the right place and alight was a constant challenge!

The advance guard of Imperial Airways arrived in Poole Harbour in September 1939, when a fleet of launches brought equipment around from Hythe. The move was completed in January 1940, when the company was amalgamated with its smaller rival, British Airways, and incorporated as a state-owned airline: British Overseas Airways Corporation. BOAC's administrative offices were installed in Airways House at No.4 Poole High Street (now Poole Museum), where they remained for the next ten years. Initially, all passenger arrival and departure facilities were provided at the Haven Hotel at Sandbanks. However, as the threat of imminent invasion brought more and more military to the area, by May 1940 the civilian flying boat operations were moved to the Quay, where Poole Pottery had been requisitioned to provide a Departure and Arrivals Hall on the ground floor and a Restaurant and Lounge on the floor above. Customs and Immigration were based at the Antelope Hotel and the Cargo Section was operated from one of the quayside pottery warehouses.

211. A BOAC passenger tender crewed by seawomen taking a flying boat crew out to the moorings, passing one of the blockships protecting Poole Quay, which can be seen in the background.

212. The Water Controller's pinnace, MCA.1316.

A fleet of launches was essential to ferry crew, passengers and cargo out to the flying boats at their moorings. These launches were all marked in the livery of British Airways Marine Services and were maintained and refuelled at the Launch House, just above the bridge on the Hamworthy side. They were built by The British Powerboat Company which moved from Southampton to Poole at about the same time, occupying sheds in West Quay Road where the RNLI now stands. BOAC had four passenger launches, two crash launches, baggage launches and several general-purpose runabouts. These were moored in the Fishermans' Dock overnight, and brought out to the Quay or Salterns Basin, as required during the day.

The Flying Boat Era

213. A crew of BOAC 'seawomen', undergoing training in launch handling under the watchful eye of an instructor on Poole Quay. As the male launch hands were called up into the services, women were trained to take their place.

In addition to BOAC's assorted craft, the Ministry of Civil Aviation had four fast launches for controlling flying and manoeuvring operations on the harbour waters. These powerful MCA vessels were capable of 20 knots and were responsible for ensuring that the runways were properly marked, clearing them of any debris, and one would be anchored in the lee of Brownsea Island to give radio clearance to incoming or outgoing craft.

As the male launch-hands gradually got called up into the services, BOAC recruited and trained women to take their place. There were eventually 18 'seawomen', who added a touch of glamour to the quayside in their uniform of blue trousers, white sweaters and naval caps. They became most proficient at handling the launches and coped well with the demanding and very physical job they were asked to do.

Throughout the war, the flying boats from Poole Harbour provided the only regular scheduled service for post and priority passengers to the farthest parts of the British Empire. Mail and freight were loaded on to launches at Poole Quay, to be ferried out to the flying-boats at their moorings. The postman, who had collected the mail from Bournemouth Central Station in his van, was required to accompany it in the launch, personally to supervise its loading aboard. Provisioning of the flying boats was also carried out from the Quay by the cabin and launch crews and the laborious business of refuelling was undertaken by a bowser launch, filled by hand-pump on Hamworthy quay and again pumped by hand into the flying boat's tanks at its moorings.

A problem for those who had to keep the Empire flying boats operational was routine maintenance. All the mechanics and their equipment had to be ferried out to the boats at their moorings, and the engineers had to work from launches tied alongside, or by climbing all over them; difficult enough on a calm day, a nightmare if it was blowing hard. More

214. Mail and freight bound for all parts of the Empire being loaded onto a launch alongside Poole Quay, to be taken out to a flying boat moored in the harbour.

215. BOAC Stewardesses on Poole Quay carry a container of insulated flasks on board a launch crewed by one of the Seawomen.

serious repairs had to be returned to Southampton Water, where the specialist maintenance depot established at Hythe in 1937 by Imperial Airways was retained during and after the war. When BOAC later acquired the huge American Boeings, they regularly had to be returned to the USA for servicing of their engines, although minor repairs could be carried out at Hythe.

The Flying Boat Era

216. A launch crewed by seawomen alongside a C-Class flying boat, with engineers working on the engines from on top of the wings.

217. Lord Wavell departing from Poole Quay in the Autumn of 1943, to take up his post as the new Viceroy of India and Supreme Commander of Allied Forces in South-East Asia.

BOAC's passengers were generally VIPs: high-ranking military personnel like Field-Marshal Sir Archibald Wavell, the new Viceroy of India, or senior foreign or Government officials; there would also be the very wealthy, and occasionally famous entertainers. Many

218. The principal
flying boat routes
during the war.
Before the war,
Imperial Airways
had established the
Horseshoe Route
from Durban to
Cairo, across India
to Australia and
New Zealand.

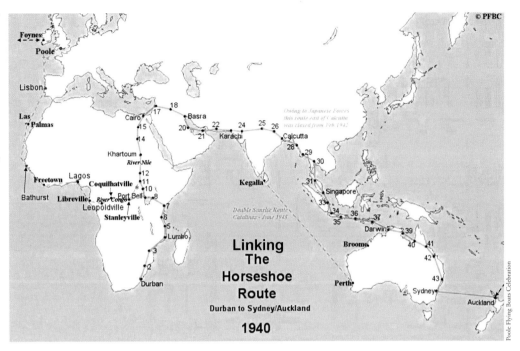

came down from London on specially-chartered trains and spent the night in the Harbour Heights Hotel, ready for an early morning departure. Some were ferried from other parts of the country in smaller planes. In the first three years of the war, outgoing passengers assembled in the Waiting Room on the Quay before being taken out by launch to the flying boat at its mooring off Salterns.

The routes taken by the flying boats to Africa and the Far East were inevitably vulnerable to the ebb and flow of hostilities. Pre-war, Imperial Airways had established a base in Durban in South Africa, from where it pioneered a service known from its shape on the map as the 'Horseshoe Route'. This ran north from South Africa via the lakes in the Rift Valley to Cairo, then across the Middle East to India, through Malaya and Burma and on to Australia and New Zealand. Flights from the UK crossed France and the Mediterranean to meet up with the Horseshoe Route at Cairo.

The fall of France and the entry of Italy into the war had serious implications for communications with the Empire, because the Mediterranean route was no longer possible. Urgent consideration was given to alternatives, and it was clear that the only suitable neutral country within range was Portugal. From Lisbon it might be possible to continue down the west coast of Africa, via Bathurst in Gambia and Lagos in Nigeria, before crossing the narrowest part of Africa to link up with the Horseshoe Route from Durban to Cairo and so on across the Middle East to India. However there was a big snag: this route would have to cross the vastness of French Equatorial Africa, which was controlled by a regime loyal to the Vichy French, no longer Britain's ally. Until this could be overcome, Great Britain would remain cut off from its Empire,

This gave rise to one of the most daring flights of the war. BOAC was in the middle of undertaking a series of proving flights across the Atlantic to the USA, using an Empire boat

219. An RAF Catalina coming in to land. This was a highly successful long range boat, of which BOAC had seven and there were many more on the harbour used by the military at their base at Hamworthy.

220. A giant Boeing 314A 'Speedbird' taking off from Poole Harbour, with the kilns of Poole Pottery in the background.

specially equipped with long-range fuel tanks. This was on its mooring in Poole harbour, waiting to take off for North America when it was diverted on a desperately dangerous mission: to fly a group of Free French army officers to the Congo in attempt to persuade local French troops to change their allegiance. Without any ground support, radio assistance or navigational aids, the flying boat landed several days later on the uncharted waters of the Congo River. Here the passengers went ashore to negotiate with the resident French Army General. A successful coup was organised and the air routes across Africa opened up to BOAC. Not only mail and passengers, but also vital supplies to British forces in Africa, could start to flow again – all within six weeks of being interrupted.

The first American plane to be added to BOAC's fleet at Poole was probably the most successful flying boat design of all time: the Catalina, built by Consolidated Aircraft of San Diego. BOAC eventually had seven Catalinas in all, but there were many more on the harbour, used by the RAF at their base at Hamworthy.

Poole Flying Boats Celebration

In 1941, BOAC purchased from America the most powerful addition to its fleet, three gigantic Boeing 314a's. These had a much greater range than Shorts' Empire boats and were operated on the North American route as a separate company, Airways Atlantic Limited. They also had a greater payload of 70 passengers and crew, although rarely did they actually carry this number; not only was mail and freight of greater importance, but also those passengers who could pull sufficient rank to be able to use the service were so important that they were given lots of space. Nevertheless, the greater range of the Boeings enabled BOAC to fly regular schedules to North America, via Foynes in neutral Ireland.

Military flying boats arrived in Poole Harbour in August 1942. Throughout that year, Britain's merchant shipping was being sunk in huge quantities by the Nazi U-Boats in the Atlantic. The military flying boats of RAF Coastal Command, particularly the Sunderland, Short's rugged anti-submarine boat which bristled with gun turrets, played a vital role in this battle. They flew long patrols from their Scottish bases out over the ocean to spot and attack submarines which had surfaced to replenish their air supply and charge their batteries. To widen the coverage of these patrols, the RAF decided to create a military flying boat base in Poole Harbour, initially called RAF Poole, but soon changed to RAF Hamworthy when it took over the WWI concrete slipways at Lake. A few private houses were requisitioned on the Lake Estate, but no purpose-built administration or maintenance buildings were erected and the ground staff had to make do with tents until they eventually acquired Dorset Yacht Company's dinghy shed as a canteen. Living accommodation was spread all over the Borough, messing facilities were in the Blue Lagoon Club and the Harbour Heights and, from January 1943, the Squadron HQ was moved from 51 Parkstone Road to the Harbour Club. Arrangements were far from ideal!

222. A Sunderland military flying boat of RAF 210 Squadron, Coastal Command, used on anti U-Boat patrols in the Atlantic. Civilian versions, known as the 'Hythe Class' were used by BOAC from 1943.

223. The Harbour Heights Hotel in Canford Cliffs served a variety of purposes during the war. In particular, it provided overnight accommodation for passengers on BOAC's flying boats, and the Officers' Mess for BOAC and RAF Hamworthy.

The first unit to be based at Hamworthy was the Royal Australian Air Force 461 Squadron with its Sunderland flying boats. They were accompanied by an RAF Marinecraft Unit with launches to take over the clearing of runways, lighting flare-paths, etc., based at Salterns Pier. The Australians were less than happy with the hastily-organised facilities in Poole and most relieved when they were relocated to Pembroke Dock in April 1943. They were soon replaced by another element of Coastal Command, RAF 210 Squadron, 'the Catalina Squadron', but by December 1943 the difficulties of operating in such a crowded harbour, coupled with the Navy's need of the slipways at Hamworthy to practise

224. The Harbour Yacht Club at Salterns which in 1943 became the flying boat operations centre & departure terminal for BOAC, as well as the Meteorological Station for both British and American forces.

225. The scene at the head of Salterns Pier, with two flying boats at their moorings. The launches are taking passengers out for an early morning departure.

Poole Flying Boats Celebration

loading landing craft, combined to have the military flying boats posted elsewhere and RAF Hamworthy was reduced to a 'Care & Maintenance' facility.

Prior to the end of 1942, the Army had been persuaded to vacate the Harbour Club at Salterns which, due to its location overlooking the moorings and main runway, was much better suited to the management of day-to-day flying boat operations. A Flying Control Centre was established on the second floor overlooking the harbour, administered jointly by the RAF and the Air Ministry, to control the movements of both military and civilian flying boats. Salterns pier was extended with the help of the Royal Engineers Experimental Bridging Unit from Christchurch, and two 'flak barges' mounted with anti-aircraft guns

226. A BOAC passenger launch disembarking passengers from a Hythe Class flying boat on its moorings off Salterns.

LANDING CARD FOR ALL PASSENGERS I.B.28

IMPORTANT. This card must be filled in by the passenger before arrival at the U.K. port.
(Ce questionnaire doit être rempli par le voyageur avant son arrivée au port de débarquement dans le Royaume Uni.)

Port of Embarkation *Poole*
(Port d'embarquement)

Surname (in block letters) *BIANCHI   FIELDS*
(Nom en caractères gros)

Christian Names *GRACE*   Occupation *ActRESS*
(Prénoms)   (Profession)

Date of birth *January 9th 1848*   Place of birth *Rochdale*   Sex *Female*
(Date de Naissance)   (Lieu de Naissance)   (Sexe)

Nationality *BRITISH*   Nationality at birth *BRITISH*   *1940*
(Nationalité)   (Nationalité de Naissance)

Passport Number *C 114426*   Place of issue *Los Angeles*   Date *July 29*
(Numéro de passeport)   (Délivré à)

Proposed address in U.K. *Drury Lane Theatre London.*
(Adresse proposée dans le Royaume Uni)

Signature *Grace Bianchi, Gracie Fields*
(Signature du voyageur)

PRESCRIBED UNDER THE ALIENS ORDER, 1920

British Overseas Airways Corporation Form No. 555B 94616

227. Landing card completed by Gracie Fields when arriving in Poole by flying boat in July 1940.

and manned by No.130 Regiment Light AA, were moored on either side of it. Guard duties were undertaken by a detachment from No.4021 Squadron RAF Regiment.

By March 1943, BOAC was able to move certain of its operations from Poole Quay to join the RAF in the Harbour Club. The original bar and dining room on the ground floor of the Harbour Club were smartly redecorated as BOAC's Departure Terminal and passengers could walk out along Jennings' pier and embark into a launch for a much shorter journey to the flying boat at its mooring. The building must have bulged at the seams, containing, as

Poole Flying Boats Celebration

it did, RAF Transport Command, the headquarters staff of RAF Hamworthy, together with their Operations, Signals, Ciphers, Intelligence and Meteorology Sections, as well as the Air Ministry staff, those from BOAC and those from the 36th Air Sea Rescue Unit whose fast boats were based in Salterns Dock. Later, as D Day approached, they were joined by the Meteorological Station of the US Navy.

Incoming passengers arriving in Poole were still taken by launch directly to Poole Quay, where Customs, Immigration and Secret Service screening facilities were by now in Poole Pottery. All passengers had to complete a landing card, and we have a copy of one for Gracie Fields in 1940. Many prominent people passed through the Poole Harbour facilities, including General De Gaulle, Lord Louis Mountbatten and Anthony Eden, although Churchill is thought never to have made it. He was due to land here on the way back from meeting Roosevelt in the USA, but an air raid at Poole diverted his flying boat to Plymouth instead.

Throughout the war so far, BOAC's civilian flying boats had frequently been diverted for use in support of military operations, and in 1943 there was pressure to regulate this by consolidating all civilian and military transport planes under the single overall control of RAF Transport Command. Unsurprisingly, BOAC objected strongly to this, and all but one of the Main Board resigned in protest. BOAC did retain control of its regular Atlantic, West Africa and Horseshoe Route operations, but all its other flying boats were given RAF Registration Numbers and were ultimately part of RAF Transport Command, which was also based at Salterns with a total of 24 flying boats at its disposal.

Only one flying boat was lost in Poole due to enemy action. This was Maia, the bottom half of the pick-a-back pair, with which Imperial Airways had been experimenting before the war, in an endeavour to ferry mail across the Atlantic in one hit. The work-horse Maia, took off with the lighter seaplane, Mercury, strapped on her back. When the fuel-consuming takeoff and maximum altitude had been achieved, the smaller plane left

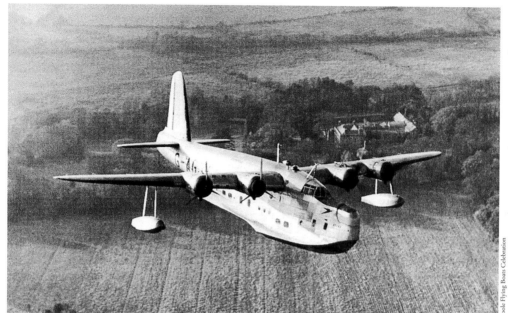

229. A Short's Hythe Class flying boat, which was a post-war adaptation of the military Sunderland for civilian use. The gun turrets have been removed, but access to the nose was still necessary when mooring the boats.

Poole Flying Boats Celebration

230. Poole Quay in the run up to D-Day, with American Coastguard cutters moored three and four deep.

her carrier and had ample fuel to take her across to North America. The war halted trials and Maia was adapted for passenger use on the shuttle route between Poole and Foynes in Southern Ireland. It was on its moorings on 12 May 1941 when a lone Heinkel bomber made a sneak raid on the harbour, scoring a near miss on Maia which damaged and slowly sank her, taking her unfortunate night-watchman with her. The Heinkel was so unwise as to come back for a second run, and was brought down in the harbour by Poole's anti-aircraft gunners.

Numerous houses were required to accommodate all the support staff for the flying boats and most of those requisitioned were in Parkstone, including a large house in Dorset

231. BOAC flying boats on their moorings off Salterns, just post-war, have to share the harbour with Dolphin dinghies from Parkstone Yacht Club.

Lake Avenue, required as a Sick Bay for the workforce which, with more than 600 people, was one of the largest employers in Poole during the war. An appendix to this chapter lists those premises known to have been used for this purpose, Many local residents with spare rooms in their homes had staff billeted on them under war-time regulations, whether they liked it or not! The Blue Lagoon Club was used as a messroom and canteen for all military personnel, including those from RAF Hamworthy.

In 1943, BOACs Empire boats were replaced by the 'Sunderland Mark III'. These were somewhat spartan civilian conversions of the military version, and BOAC eventually had a total of 24. Their flights continued throughout the rest of the war, and the only time they were interrupted was in May 1944, in the run-up to D-Day, when all flying operations were moved temporarily to Pembroke Dock, to make room for the build-up of warships and landing-craft in the harbour. BOAC returned to Poole in September.

With the surrender of the Japanese in the Far East in 1945, flying boats were sent out from Poole to help repatriate some of the more desperately ill emerging from the prison camps. It was felt that a sea voyage back to the UK with good food would help restore those in reasonable shape, but others needed urgent hospital attention. The arrival of these emaciated skeletons had a traumatic affect on BOAC crews, both on board the boats and when they were unloaded into the passenger launches to be taken to Poole Quay. The reaction of one young seawoman is preserved in an emotional recording which can be heard in Poole Museum. She recounts how, as they gently laid the stretcher containing the emaciated body of a young man on the cabin roof of the launch, he looked round at the harbour and said faintly "Oh, how lovely to be home."... and then died.

As the war came to an end, and sailing was permitted in the harbour once again, the giant flying boats had to share the water with those dinghies and yachts that had survived the war intact. Although there was great joy at the ending of hostilities, it was still a time of

232. In 1954 the flying boat 'Southampton' returned to Poole and is here moored off Hamworthy.

Poole Flying Boats Celebration

233. No longer wanted, the flying boats were taken ashore on the beach at Hamworthy to be broken up for scrap. They became an exciting adventure playground for many local school children.

Leslie Dawson

austerity, and there was little money about for flying anywhere, unless you were on official business. BOAC had been using landplanes from RAF Hurn for several years, and now that the traditional Mediterranean routes were open again, these were proving faster and more economical than the great flying boats. London Airport was under construction at the suburban village of Heath Row immediately post-war and, as soon as it was ready, it became the UK's main airport.

After the war ended, BOAC was issued with Short's 'Hythe Class' flying boats which were a rather more luxurious adaptation of the reliable Sunderland, aimed at the tourist market. They were trying to drum up business from wealthy travellers and holidaymakers, and a local man recalls that, as a schoolboy, he was taken out by his father in about 1947 to see one of these flying boat off Salterns, and was very impressed by the red plush seats. The airline was offering return flights to Malta, including the two nights hotel accommodation en route, for 19 guineas.

On 31st March 1948, BOAC moved its flying boat terminal back to Southampton, where more convenient along-side mooring facilities were provided, to eliminate the launch journeys. However the days of scheduled flying boat operations in the UK were coming to an end as the land planes took over, and the airline eventually ceased all scheduled services in November 1950. Although a separate private company, Aquila Airways, tried to keep the flying boat era alive, it failed and closed in September 1958. An era had come to an end.

During its time in Poole, BOAC had made more than 5000 flights from the harbour. These magnificent machines, and the extraordinary men who flew them, had kept open our communications with the vast British Empire, on which we had relied so heavily to win the war. And there are still many elderly Poole residents who remember clearly the roar of four mighty propeller-driving engines as the massive machines came in low over Sandbanks to land in the main channel. Soon however there was silence over the harbour as air traffic moved first to Hurn and then to Heath Row. However, flying-boats did come back to Poole again in the mid 1950s, and many remember them lying on moorings off Hamworthy ; sadly it was only for them to be taken ashore to be broken up on the beach**.**

234. The glory days! A flying boat touches down after an overseas flight.

The Flying Boat Era

List of properties in Parkstone known to have been requisitioned for flying boat or seaplane purposes, 1939 – 1945.

(These do not include Poole Quay or Hamworthy, and there may well have been others.)

Brudennel House, Brudennel Road	*Officers Mess Staff*
Flats 1,2,3,5 & 6, Harbour Court, Canford Cliffs	*Officers Quarters*
Bransdene, Brudennel Avenue	*WAAF Officers Quarters*
Folly Cottage, Dorset Lake Avenue, Lilliput	*Station Sick Quarters*
Stretton Court, Castle Hill, Parkstone	*WAAF Hostel & Mess*
Merrion, Castle Hill, Parkstone	*WAAF Hostel*
Varenne, Springfield Road, Parkstone	*WAAF Hostel*
Parkstone Motor Co Garage, Station Road	*Motor Transport Centre*
Bethshalom, Sandbanks Road, Parkstone	
Elms Cottage, Sandbanks Road, Parkstone	
5 Elgin Road, Parkstone	*Stores Ration*
High Trees, Elms Avenue, Parkstone	
The Blue Lagoon Club & Cafe, Sandbanks Road	*Airman's Mess*
Flats 10 & 15 Salterns Court, Lilliput	
Blue Peter, Salterns Way, Lilliput	
Harbour Cottage, Salterns Way, Lilliput	*Staff Hostel*
Moss Agate, Salterns Way, Lilliput	
Whatley House, Salterns Way, Lilliput	
The Harbour Yacht Club, Salterns Way, Lilliput	
Kathryn, Brownsea View Avenue, Lilliput	
The Arches, Anthony's Avenue, Lilliput	*Stores Equipment*
White Ladies, Anthony's Avenue, Lilliput	
Crichel Place & Knoll Lodge, Lilliput	*Sergeants' Mess*
Winthorpe, Alington Road, Lilliput	*Sergeants' Mess*
Rowena, Elms Avenue, Lilliput	*WAAF Catering staff*
Salterns Court, Sandbanks Road, Lilliput	*Office of C.O., & Station HQ*
Blue Peter, Salterns Way, Lilliput	*Station Accounts Section, NAAFI*
Grayrigg, Crichel Mount Road	
32 Austin Avenue, Lilliput	*Medical Officer's accommodation*
Mount House, Mount Road, Seaview	*WRNS Hostel*
Tangley	
Ivanhoe	
Holmdale	
Lalbagh	*WAAF Hostel*
Harbour Heights Hotel, Haven Road	*Officers Mess & passenger accommodation*
RMYC, Panorama Road, Sandbanks	*Fleet Air Arm Training school*
Sandbanks Yacht Co. Yard, Sandbanks	*Seaplane base*
10 Old Coastguard Road	*FAA Guardroom*
Fowey Cottage, 44 Panorama Road	*Sickbay*
Cama, Panorama Road, Sandbanks	*Ratings Quarters*
The Moorings, Panorama Road	*Ratings Quarters*
Belle Holme, Panorama Road	*Petty Officers Mess*
Red House, Brownsea Road	*WRNS Mess*
Byfleet, Panorama Road, Sandbanks	*Ratings Quarters*

Chapter 15

The Seaplanes

Another war-time user of the harbour was the Fleet Air Arm with its seaplanes. The Navy used seaplanes for a wide variety of purposes: for search and rescue at sea, for spotting enemy ships, and for torpedo attacks. Some were flown from aircraft carriers, such as the *"Illustrious"* or *"Ark Royal"*. Many were carried as deck cargo on large vessels such as battleships, cruisers or armed merchant ships, from which the planes would be launched by catapult. They would then hope to be recovered by crane after they had landed in the sea – it all seemed very risky, and those pilots must have prayed for calm conditions! But it is clear that that additional skills were required of these pilots, over and above their land-based training, so the Navy had specialised training squadrons for this purpose.

Before the war, all training took place at the headquarters of the Fleet Air Arm. This was a Naval airfield known as HMS Daedalus, the Royal Naval Air Station at Lee-on-Solent, which had a slipway into the water for amphibious aircraft. However, with increased war-time shipping and other military activities, as well as the risk of German bombing, it was decided to move the training element of their operation to quieter and safer locations. In 1940, 765 Squadron was sent to Poole to what was to become known officially as "HMS Daedalus II", but was referred to affectionately by many locals as "HMS Tadpole". The seaplanes, in contrast to the huge flying boats, were regarded as "tiddlers". The following year 764 Squadron was relocated to RNAS Lawrenny Ferry, just upstream from Pembroke Dock in Wales.

In July 1940, an advance party of Naval officers from Lee on Solent arrived to prepare for the transfer of 765 Squadron to Sandbanks, where they based themselves at the Royal Motor Yacht Club. One of them was a young Surgeon-Lieutenant, Ronald Pitts Crick. Only recently qualified, he was to be the Station's Medical Officer. Later in his career he became a most eminent eye-specialist, practising in Kent. However, he so enjoyed his posting that, after the war, he bought a home on Sandbanks to which he eventually retired. He became a member of the Royal Motor Yacht Club, and a number of the photographs were his.

This advance guard set about obtaining the facilities that the Air Station would need to operate effectively. They first requisitioned the RMYC club building for use as the Wardroom. Then the Poole Harbour Yacht Company's boatshed next door, and Sandbanks Yacht Company's boatyard just down the road, were acquired; both were needed for the storage and servicing of aircraft. An immediate problem was that both boatsheds were packed with private yachts, carefully stored away by club members for the duration of the war. The Navy had to employ local fishermen to launch them, tow them over beyond

Ronald Pitts Crick

235. Surgeon-Lieutenant Ronald Pitts Crick, left, and fellow officers outside the front door of HMS Daedalus II (the Royal Motor Yacht Club) in 1941.

Goathorn into the back reaches of the harbour and beach them all.

In addition to the commercial premises, the Navy also requisitioned various houses: No.10 Coastguard Cottages, which now fronts the yacht club car-park, was the guardhouse and lock-up; "Fowey Cottage", almost next door in Panorama Road, was acquired as a sick bay and "The Moorings" at 118 Panorama Road accommodated the eight pilots in training at any one time; two other houses in Panorama Road, "Cama" and "Byfleet", were used as living accommodation for Ratings (the latter was destroyed by a stray bomb in 1942, but fortunately all personnel were at lunch in the canteen in the Haven Hotel at the time). The "Red House" in Brownsea Road was acquired as a Wren's accommodation unit and Mess, and the Haven Hotel was the general Military Command Centre for the area.

The Royal Naval Air Station, Sandbanks, was commissioned on 26th August 1940. Initially 765 Squadron had 12 seaplanes, together with a further six designated for 766 Squadron and taken on loan. A photograph taken of the members of the Ship's Company soon after the station was set up shows exactly 100 people, although the complement reached 120 later, mainly with additional Wrens, as a result of the conscription of women in 1941. That was quite a lot of people for whom accommodation had to be found at short notice. They are photographed outside Poole Harbour Yacht Company's boatshed, which was used for servicing engines and repairs. The interior today still carries a reminder of the seaplanes' occupation. On the wall is painted this warning sign: "A HOT ENGINE IS ALWAYS ON CONTACT".

236. The Royal Motor Yacht Club premises, bottom right, next to the works of the Poole Harbour Yacht Co., with the yard and pier of the Sandbanks Yacht Company beyond, taken just pre-war. All of these were requisitioned by the Fleet Air Arm in 1940 as a seaplane training base, formally known as HMS Daedalus II, Royal Naval Air Station, Sandbanks.

237. The staff of HMS Daedalus II, taken outside what is now the RMYC boatshed, soon after the station was commissioned.

Apart from repairing the Club pier, blown up by the Army at the start of the war to prevent its use by the expected German invasion, the Navy personnel carried out other works to enable proper use of the new Air Station. They laid a substantial concrete slipway to allow the seaplanes to be hauled out of the water. They installed fuel tanks to hold 4000 gallons of aviation fuel in the boatyard, and built two air-raid shelters, one in the yard just outside the yacht club, and the other further down Panorama Road at Number 100, which is still there today; these were for use by both military personnel and those civilians still living on Sandbanks. They also had their own fire engine and trained crew.

The Seaplanes

238. A seaplane is hauled ashore for servicing on the slipway at RNAS Sandbanks in about 1942.

Royal Motor Yacht Club

The main role of the instructors of 765 Squadron was to take pilots who had already learnt to fly conventional aircraft and put them through the "Basic Seaplane Course", which usually took two weeks. It was also necessary to familiarise them with the various types of aircraft that they might be required to fly. To do this, the base was equipped with a cross-section of the seaplanes used by the Navy. Initially the most numerous were the Supermarine Walrus, designed by Reginald Mitchell of Spitfire fame. The Walrus had an undercarriage as well as floats, so could come down on either land or water. It was known to the pilots as the "Shagbat", and was used for spotting enemy ships and reconnaissance, as well as patrol, search and rescue, and communications duties.

Another old faithful was the Fairey Swordfish, affectionately known as the "Stringbag". This was a versatile, but old-fashioned biplane, which had a wheeled undercarriage which was easily interchangeable with floats. It was used particularly as a spotter aircraft aboard battleships and cruisers and as a torpedo bomber from aircraft carriers. It has gone down in history for the brave but suicidal torpedo attack on the German battle fleet when it made its dash through the English Channel in 1942, when all six of our planes were lost. It will also be remembered for the highly successful torpedo attack which crippled the Bismarck and eventually led to its sinking. Another Fairey design was the Seafox, which had the reputation of being somewhat underpowered. Towards the end of 1942, these began to be replaced by the American-built Kingfisher, which had an unconventional central float. Later, in the summer of 1943, the prototype of the Supermarine Sea Otter arrived, which was intended to be the replacement of the good old workhorse, the Walrus. This seaplane had a traditional pulling propeller, rather than the "pusher" on the Walrus.

The Royal Navy, advised by the RAF and Imperial Airways, had already established and

239. A
Supermarine
Walrus seaplane
taxis ashore on
the Sandbanks
slipway in
1941.

Poole Flying Boats Celebration

240. A Fairey
Swordfish in
flight, carrying
torpedo.

Poole Flying Boats Celebration

marked several runways on Poole Harbour for the use of both flying-boats and seaplanes. The seaplanes were allocated the runway down Sou' Deep, although they also used one to the north of Brownsea Island, if the wind direction dictated it. Both seaplane and flying boat movements were controlled by radio communications based at The Harbour Club at Salterns. Seaplane moorings were mainly along the Wych Channel, in the lee of Brownsea.

Poole Flying Boats Celebration

241. A Kingfisher seaplane taking off from Poole Harbour in 1943 with, in the background, Poole Quay and four Catalina flying boats from RAF 210 Squadron on their moorings.

Poole harbour during the war presented a very different picture from today's maze of boats and moorings. The main body of the harbour had been entirely cleared of civilian vessels, and the only buoys marked the flying-boat and seaplane runways. The movements of cargo ships, military craft, flying boats and seaplanes were monitored and controlled by the Harbour Controller in a large motor pinnace.

No.765 Squadron at RNAS Sandbanks was, of course, a training squadron, putting pilots through the watery equivalent of "circuits and bumps", and, from all reports, there were indeed some bumps. Many of the incidents were relatively minor, when inexperienced pilots collided with boats, buoys or piers, probably having failed to make allowances for the strong tides, or for the wind. If a rookie pilot had managed to collect debris hanging from the wings, the ground-staff would disparagingly describe him as returning *"decorated for Christmas"*!

One Walrus was damaged going aground on Stone Island, a shingle bank near the harbour entrance, and others were damaged when their undercarriage collapsed as they were pulled ashore. No one was killed in training, and the ground crews became expert in servicing and patching up minor damage, but at least two aircraft were entirely written off by landing errors, and several seriously damaged. In 1943, when the harbour was becoming very congested with the build-up of assault craft prior to the invasion of Europe, one Walrus apparently disgraced itself by colliding with a flying-boat off Salterns pier.

Although Sandbanks was considerably safer than Lee-on-Solent, it was not entirely safe from enemy action. A 1940 German reconnaissance photo taken of the harbour shows that the Luftwaffe were aware of several important targets in the area, including Poole Docks and the flying-boat Marine Terminal at Salterns. However, of greatest strategic importance

242. The Fleet Air Arm training base at the RMYC in about 1943, with two naval ratings and a small tender in front of the boatshed.

was the huge munitions factory at Holton Heath, at the west end of the harbour, and all of these targets were attacked on several occasions. Brownsea Island was equipped as one of three local 'Star Fish' sites, designed as a decoy, with massive tanks of oil which could be set alight electrically to mislead the enemy bombers. One stray bomb from such an attack did destroy the house on Sandbanks used as the ratings dormitory, though fortunately no-one was in it at the time.

In addition to training, the Squadron's role included "air search and rescue" (ASR) in the Channel: looking for the crews of downed RAF planes and landing to pick them up, if conditions allowed, or reporting their position to the RAF's own fast motor boats. Within the first month of arriving at Sandbanks, the realities of war were brought home to all personnel: Lieutenant Tommy Rose-Richards, famous as one of the dare-devil racing drivers at Brooklands pre-war, and his observer, Mike Hoskins, were in an unarmed Walrus, looking for a downed aircraft a few miles off Swanage. They were attacked by enemy fighters, and both were killed.

On another occasion, Surgeon-Lieutenant Pitts Crick had a narrow escape just outside the yacht club gates when the base was strafed by a Messerschmitt long-range fighter on a sneak attack. His presence of mind in diving behind a concrete plinth saved his bacon.

The Fleet Air Arm's stay in Sandbanks was relatively short-lived. As the war developed, the demand for seaplane pilots reduced considerably, and the decision to disband both training squadrons was taken in the latter part of 1943. On 25th October that year, 765 Squadron was disbanded. The Sandbanks station was reduced to a 'care and maintenance' role, manned by a skeleton staff under the wing of HMS Turtle, the Combined Operations Establishment at Hamworthy. It saw a brief flurry of activity when its facilities were used by

The Seaplanes

American staff as part of the Combined Ops, together with a landing-craft unit based there, in the build-up to D Day, but never returned to full operational use.

The life of HMS Tadpole was a short one, but a merry one – or perhaps, more accurately, a comfortable one, because several of those who served there remember it as their most luxurious posting of the war! Others recall, perhaps with a touch of guilt, the friendly ladies in one of the adjacent Coastguard Cottages who, for a price, provided solace for lonely servicemen when off duty!

The Royal Motor Yacht Club eventually got its premises back on 31st July 1945. Thanks to the various wartime occupants, particularly the Navy, it was in relatively good condition, so it was able to open its doors to members again within a month. Yachting in all its forms has continued there ever since.

243. Troops from the Royal Engineers laying barbed wire defences on Sandbanks beach.

Chapter 16

Parkstone at War

In the First World War there had been relatively little change to the daily lives of local residents. Certainly women were then for the first time working in factories and other occupations previously the preserve of men; Naval and commercial shipping traffic in the harbour increased enormously and, as we have seen at Salterns, there was extensive development for war-related industry. Above all, the conscription and loss of so many young men affected almost every family. However, in the Second World War, destruction and death came to Parkstone, as it did to all other parts of the Borough.

In the first few months of the war, the Nazi armies ruthlessly and efficiently over-ran all opposition in northern Europe, occupying Poland, Denmark, Norway, Holland and Belgium, before launching their attack on France. This met with the same success, leading to the defeat of the combined French and British forces and the retreat from Dunkirk in May 1940. By mid June the French Government had sued for peace, leaving German troops in control of the coast just across the Channel from Southern England. Major English cities were now within 30 minutes flying time of German bombers, and a cross-Channel invasion within weeks was seen as inevitable.

244. Troops from the Green Howards man a newly-built defence position on Poole's shoreline.

Poole Historical Trust

Parkstone at War

Poole Historical Trust

245. *Foxholes dug into the sandy clifftop of Poole Head, in front of the Camouflage Training School along Chaddesley Wood Road, during 1940.*

Feverish activity gripped the authorities all along the South Coast, no more so than in Poole, because the beaches between Hurst Castle and Studland seemed to offer the most obvious landing ground for any invading force. Travel restrictions were put in place all along the coast, and Poole was declared a 'Defence Area' with access limited to residents and authorised persons only. The Royal Engineers erected barbed wire entanglements and anti-landing barricades all along the shores of Poole Bay, piers and jetties were destroyed to prevent their use by an invasion force, and civilians were prohibited access to '*the seashore, sandhills or outmarsh*' of Hampshire and Dorset. Fortified gun emplacements were constructed along the coast, and beach huts removed to give better lines of fire.

In June 1940 The Queen's Bays, who had been stationed in Poole, were posted to the Middle East, to be replaced by the 7th Battalion of The Green Howards. They had miraculously escaped from Dunkirk, but had had to leave virtually all their weapons and equipment behind. They dug in along the coast, particularly at Sandbanks. Numerous buildings were requisitioned by the authorities for use by the military or other organisations, and the existing owners and occupiers could do little about it. During 1938, in anticipation of the coming war, the Directorate of Lands and Accommodation within the Ministry of Works had set up a central register of accommodation, which was used during and after the war for identifying and requisitioning land and buildings required for the war effort by any military or civil service department. The powers for any requisition stemmed from the Defence (General) Regulations 1939 made under the Emergency Powers (Defence) Act 1939. It was recognised that dispossessed owners had to be compensated, and this was calculated under the terms of the Compensation (Defence) Act 1939. In effect, the requisitioning authority knocked on your door, gave you a deadline to leave, and you were left to agree lease terms with the Ministry of Works in due course.

In Parkstone, each building requisitioned might house a whole range of organisations;

amongst them was the Sandbanks Hotel which was the base for Southern Command's School of Vehicle Maintenance and its Infantry Training School, the Haven Hotel which formed the area's Army Operations Centre, as well as supporting the Royal Naval Signals Station at Dune Crest in Banks Road; and Sandecotes School which at one time housed the 2nd Battalion of Grenadier Guards and later US Infantry prior to D-Day. The Harbour Heights became the Officers' Mess for the RAF and BOAC and accommodated passengers overnight. The Royal Motor Yacht Club was occupied by the Seaplane Training School of the Fleet Air Arm and the Blue Lagoon Club was throughout the war a services canteen and rest centre. The Harbour Club at Salterns, with its sheltered dock, was first occupied by the army. It has been difficult to establish its precise uses during the first three years of the war, other than it was probably used by the Green Howards and was also a base for the training of what were initially called the Local Defence Volunteers, but soon became the Home Guard. By mid 1942, it was occupied by the 76th Medium Battery of the Royal Yorkshire Artillery, 38th Division, and in January 1943, after some months of extensive renovation, was handed over to the RAF and BOAC.

The Harbour Club would certainly have played a vital role in Poole's first taste of the brutal reality of war. Early in May, Germany invaded the Low Countries, and within a few days a motley fleet of overcrowded small craft carrying refugees converged on Poole Harbour, shepherded by Naval vessels. Desperate, bedraggled and with very few possessions, they were landed temporarily on Brownsea Island whilst they were sorted, screened to establish whether any were potential spies (and, indeed, two infiltrators were identified and eventually executed), and until the authorities decided what to do with them. At very short notice the army had to ferry out to Brownsea all the equipment to construct a tented camp for 3000 people, and charitable organisations throughout Poole rallied round and provided cooking utensils, bedding, clothes and the bare necessities of life.

247. Winston Churchill inspecting a pill-box at Sandbanks on his tour of the South Coast defences with General Brooke in July 1940. Part of this structure is still in place, used as a garden-room in the house next to the ferry.

On 1st July Identity Cards and Ration Books for food and fuel were issued across the country. In Poole, the Officer Commanding troops in the area designated Sandbanks a 'Restricted Military Zone'. Armed control points were put in place at The Haven and at Shore Road, all 544 residents were photographed and issued with military passes and no guests or casual visitors were permitted. Piers and landing stages were destroyed to frustrate the expected seaborne invasion, and parks, sports grounds and the fairways of Parkstone Golf Club soon sprouted rows of sawn-off telegraph poles to obstruct possible landings by airborne troops. Gun pits for anti-aircraft batteries were dug at strategic points across the Borough, including Poole Park, Whitecliff, Sandbanks and the golf course, and their munitions were stored in a bunker at Parkstone Yacht Club and under the cover of the trees on the Elms Estate.

The Battle of Britain raged in the skies over Southern England, buying valuable time to prepare our defences. On 17th July 1940 Winston Churchill drove with General Brooke, Officer Commanding the Home Forces, to inspect those defences between Gosport and Wareham. At Branksome Chine and Sandbanks he inspected pill-boxes under construction and, encouraged by the men doing the building, laid a few bricks (one of which was immediately 'liberated' and for many years was used as a door-stop in the Borough Engineer's office, before ending up in the Museum). The official party then continued on its way, ending up in Wool late that evening. The General and the Prime Minister were in agreement that it could only be a matter of a few weeks before an invasion was launched. However, the failure of the Luftwaffe to gain superiority in the air delayed Germany's invasion plans, and the approach of winter reduced the threat for the time being. Hitler turned to a bombing campaign.

In January 1941, Poole was attacked on six occasions with incendiary bombs, damaging almost 250 homes in Lilliput, Canford Cliffs, Elms Estate and Hamworthy. As a result, new Regulations required all men aged between 16 and 60 to put in 48 hours a week in fire-fighting duties, and Poole eventually had some 17,000 trained men enrolled. The Corporation took over the Sandacres Hotel to give temporary shelter to those whose houses had been bombed. On at least one occasion the hotel also housed East End families displaced by the London blitz. Boy Scouts were deputed to help them settle in, and one of these recalls the problem they had trying to round up these rough tough kids; they had never seen the sea before and had negotiated all the barbed wire and anti-landing devices at Shore Road to go paddling where it was strictly off limits!

Another major incendiary attack came on 10th April, causing widespread damage throughout the Borough, including a direct hit on the Canford Cliffs Hotel. Although a crew from the Auxiliary Fire Service reached the hotel, there was no water in the mains due to demand from the lower parts of the town, and it had to be allowed to burn to the ground. The next day, the Royal Engineers defused eight bombs in Haven Road which had failed to go off. In March and April alone, there were 88 air raid warnings, and residents had to get used to having their sleep disturbed by German bombers. On the majority of occasions these were just passing overhead on the way to other targets, or were laying mines in the approaches to Poole Harbour.

An ingenious idea spared Poole from the heaviest bombing raid of the war. The authorities were well aware that the area offered important targets: not only the vital docks and the BOAC base, but at the western end of the harbour was the Naval Cordite Factory at Holton Heath. It was decided to construct three 'Star Fish' (as in 'Special Fires') decoy sites: one at Maryland on Brownsea Island to safeguard Poole and two at Arne to protect the Cordite Factory. With the help of pyrotechnic experts from Elstree Film Studios, oil-filled storage tanks with electrical firing devices were set up at the western end of the island, and concrete bomb shelters built for the Naval technicians who would have the unenviable job of calling down the bombs on their own heads! On the 24th May 1942, more than 50 German bombers attacked Poole and the decoy was deployed. Its deliberate fires attracted 95% of the high explosive bomb load onto and around the island. A stray bomb damaged 'Byfleet' in Panorama Road, and in Hamworthy seven people were killed and 20 houses destroyed, but overall the decoy had been extraordinarily effective. German radio boasted next day that the "*Naval and Air base of Poole*" had been successfully destroyed!

Despite the incendiary attacks, Poole escaped with relatively light bomb damage when compared with other ports along the South Coast. One raid, however, had a lasting effect on the lagoon. The Luftwaffe had realised from their aerial reconnaissance that the Harbour Club and its pier were being used by the flying boats. These were attacked in the spring of 1942. A stick of five bombs fell either side of the main building, leaving it unscathed but blowing a large gap in the breakwater around the lagoon. This is still the gap where the tide, and the yachts, come and go today. The remnants of the old Sluice gates which controlled the water level in the lagoon can still be seen a few yards to the west of the new entrance.

Parkstone YC appears to have escaped being requisitioned during the war, and the 150 yachts and dinghies stored ashore were not disturbed, although the yard is believed to have been used for maintenance of RAF launches. There was a concrete pill-box on the shore

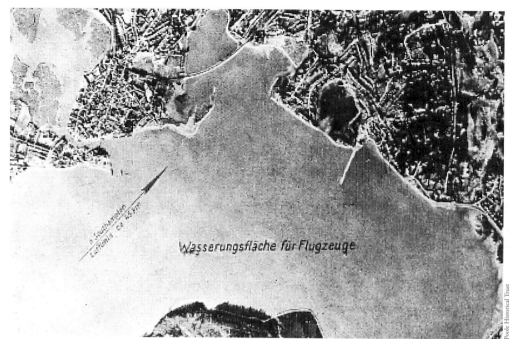

248. An extract from a reconnaissance photograph taken by the Luftwaffe in 1940, which explicitly notes the "landing area for Flying Boats"; it also clearly shows Poole docks and the Harbour Club and pier at Salterns.

by the main pier, and a substantial concrete ammunition bunker for the adjacent 40mm Bofors anti-aircraft gun. These AA gunners were given permission to use the clubhouse at night, as were the local Home Guard, probably

249. The Poole Harbour Defence Launch in 1942.

because their Commanding Officer was a club committee member.

The harbour during the war was a very different place from the conditions we know today. At the outbreak of war, it had been cleared of all private boats except those of commercial fisherman and those which had been requisitioned for military use. It was under the control of the "Naval Officer i/c Poole", based ashore at HMS Turtle at Hamworthy or on Round Island, and afloat in the Harbour Defence Launch. His role was to control shipping traffic, as well as to create the defences of the harbour. This included the provision of two substantial block-ships, loaded with explosive and positioned to block the main channel in the event of an invasion; the laying of anti-submarine nets and the creation of a mined boom across the harbour entrance; arranging sentry ships outside the entrance to check incoming vessels; organising armed harbour patrols and installing anti-landing obstructions in all shallow backwaters. The Germans regularly laid mines in the harbour approaches, and these too had to be cleared because vital inshore freighter traffic was being used intensively: there could often be a dozen or more ships alongside the quays at any one

250. A war-time aerial photograph of Poole Harbour, showing naval vessels in the foreground alongside West Quay and its various boatyards. The two blockships appear still to be held in readiness on the outer quays and, opposite Parkstone Bay, three Catalina flying boats are moored alongside the North Channel. Otherwise the harbour is cleared of moorings, apart from those marking the flying boat landing areas.

time. Virtually every vessel which would float was requisitioned for military purposes.

Eventually the tide of war turned slowly in favour of the Allies, and the harbour became even more busy and congested. It was designated an 'Invasion Base' and was the focus of the construction of all the various types of Landing Craft – those to carry infantry, or tanks or missile launchers - which local shipyards were turning out at an extraordinary rate; others were brought round under tow from Southampton and elsewhere. Numbers had reached over 300 when the RAF brought in a number of high speed launches to reinforce the Air-Sea Rescue service at Salterns pier. In addition, there were always a variety of vessels in port to be modified or repaired. The Berthing Officer was finding it harder and harder to find space for them all. There was a little bit of leeway in mid 1943 when the Fleet Air Arm seaplanes left the harbour, and Combined Ops. immediately moved 38 of their smaller landing-craft into the Sandbanks premises they vacated.

All these vessels were not just static: it was the role of HMS Turtle at Hamworthy to train troops to use them, so they were regularly going out of the harbour in large numbers to practice beach landings at Studland, or for firing practice on the Naval ranges, and the crews were given intensive training in handling these cumbersome craft. The skipper of one such LCT (Landing Craft Tank) was the author, William Golding.

In the approach to D-Day, the Catalina Squadron of RAF Coastal Command at RAF Hamworthy was moved out to allow their concrete slipways to be used to practise loading tanks onto the landing craft. Since the beginning of 1943, the Ministry of Civil Aviation had moved its control base for BOAC's flying boats to Salterns, and there were always their

251. Part of the massive build-up of landing craft in Poole Harbour, prior to the D-Day invasion. These, built by the British Power Boat Company's (No.2) Boatyard, are moored in Holes Bay.

launches going to and fro, as well as the RAF launches servicing the buoys and flarepaths. Then, in May 1944, the US Navy arrived with its fleet of 60 Coastguard Cutters, each 83 feet long. The several hundred US crewmen were bivouacked around the Borough in readiness; games of baseball could be seen being played in Whitecliff. A Free French Tank Regiment was secreted in the pine woods above the clay pits in Parkstone and US light aircraft to be used as spotter planes were stored in Poole Park and around Panorama Road in Sandbanks. The harbour and its surrounds were reaching capacity!

The harbour was a constant hive of activity, with many different branches of the military carrying out rehearsals for their particular role: It was on one such busy afternoon, when all were returning from exercises, that the incoming BOAC flight from Lisbon was due. The Water Controller did his best to clear the runway, but received a fairly salty response from the Navy to the effect that the Senior Service made way for no-one. The incoming pilot was requested by radio to make a dummy approach first, and the effect of the enormous flying boat passing overhead at mast height proved persuasive, and on the next run it was able to set down safely. A month before D-Day, BOAC moved to Neyland, near to RAF Pembroke Dock so Poole Harbour was clear for invasion traffic.

The danger from bombing had not gone away and, while there were fewer massive raids, there were numerous smaller 'hit and run' attacks like that in early 1943 by four Messerschmitt fighter-bombers which destroyed a wing of the Sandbanks Hotel, killing one Royal Marine and injuring 13 others. Poole's final air raid of the war was on 23rd April 1944 by a fleet of 70 bombers, which killed three and made 13 families homeless.

Those up early on the 6th June 1944 lined the clifftop at Canford Cliffs to watch part of the largest invasion fleet ever assembled pour out of Poole and the Solent, bound for the beaches of Normandy. For a short time there was an uncanny calm in the harbour, soon to be broken by the return of damaged craft and injured personnel. Then it was the responsibility of the Ferry services to work day and night to reinforce the troops in France

252. An enthusiastic crowd on the Quay watches the Mayor welcome home the first prisoners of war to be released from Japanese prison camps, flown home to Poole by flying boat.

with all the supplies they needed to continue the campaign: Their constant shuttle back and forth kept all the South Coast ports continuously busy, lasting till only a few weeks before the end of the war in Europe.

VE Day on the 8th May 1945 was celebrated with much spontaneous enthusiasm on Poole Quay, with all the boats dressed overall, but due to the town's close links with the Far East, the biggest victory celebrations were saved for VJ Day in August. Parkstone's principal party took place on Constitution Hill, with bonfires, flags and fireworks. However, after that, life was something of an anti-climax until mid-September when prisoners-of-war who had been held by the Japanese in the Far East began arriving home, many of them transported by flying boat to Poole. The first to arrive here were brought ashore at Poole Quay to be greeted by a huge crowd of well-wishers.

The immediate post-war years were to be a dreadful disappointment to those who had suffered so much hardship and were now hoping for the better life that everyone believed would follow victory. Rationing was still in force and indeed became more stringent. Coal, petrol, food and clothing were all in short supply, even if one had the cash and sufficient ration coupons to permit their purchase. There was a desperate need for new housing because much of the housing stock had suffered bomb damage, and there was all the residue of war to remove: barbed wire and mines to be cleared from the beaches, public parks to restore after use as allotments, air-raid shelters, pill-boxes, etc., to be removed and the harbour to be cleared of obstructions. The euphoria of victory was soon to be forgotten in the sheer struggle to make ends meet, and cope with a succession of severe winters. It was to be five more dreary years before all rationing ended and Parkstone, together with the rest of Britain, could really start to look forward to a brighter future.

Parkstone at War

253. Dolphin dinghies from Parkstone Yacht Club racing just post-war, passing two flying boats moored off Salterns.

254. Lilliput shops just post-war, before BOAC moved back to Hythe in 1948. The signboard on the right announces the company's presence. Car parking is obviously easier than today!

Chapter 17

Post-War Parkstone

In the period immediately after the Second World War, with rationing and Building Licenses still in force, Parkstone saw relatively little new development. Premises which had been requisitioned for military use during the war were handed back to their owners – usually somewhat the worse for wear! The Navy had treated the Royal Motor Yacht Club with some respect and the club was able to open again for the use of its members within a few months. However, the Blue Lagoon Club, the various hotels and numerous private houses had claims for dilapidations caused by the military occupation, and it took some time before these were all able to get back to a normal life.

After much pressure from local yacht clubs, the Naval Authorities eventually gave permission in February 1945 for sailing to resume in the harbour, although BOAC's take-off and landing schedules did lead to some heart-stopping moments as private yachts and fishing boats shared the same water as the huge flying boats. These became an attraction for sightseeing trips on the local pleasure boats.

BOAC continued to operate regular civilian flights from Poole Harbour for three years after the end of the war, once again being able to cross the Mediterranean to Alexandria on its way to the Far East. However, land-based planes were now beginning to prove more popular with the airlines, due to their greater speed and economy, and RAF Hurn briefly became the country's principal international civilian airport, operating BOAC's land planes in the period before the construction of London Airport [now called Heathrow] was completed after the war.

BOAC did not leave Poole Harbour until 1948, when flying boat operations were moved back to their base at Hythe on Southampton Water which they had originally occupied for a brief couple of years before 1939. Here they were based until flying boat operations were suspended entirely in 1950, so in fact these magnificent machines spent almost ten years based in Poole, as against a total of only four at Hythe.

After BOAC left the Harbour Club, the premises were bought by a wealthy entrepreneur called John Clark. His intention was eventually to redevelop the site but, realising it would take a long time to achieve the necessary consents, he first set about making it produce some interim income. He created the Poole Harbour Yacht Club by carrying out a superficial renovation of the building and improving the facilities. It provided an excellent dining room and members bar, a billiard room, squash court and refurbished bedrooms

Jennings' old pier was used to store and launch dinghies, but the only sheltered

255. The Poole Harbour Yacht Club, soon after its creation in 1948, when BOAC had vacated the building to return to Hythe.

256. When the flying boats left in 1948, Jennings old pier at Salterns provided facilities for the members of the new PHYC to store and launch dinghies. Initially there were no moorings along either side of the pier itself.

Poole Flying Boats Celebration

257. Concrete barges or 'caissons' which had been used in the construction of the Mulberry Harbour on D-Day were sunk in position on the east side of the PHYC pier, to increase the number of sheltered berths.

258. This aerial photo of the Poole Harbour Yacht Club shows the Mulberry Harbour caissons sunk in position to provide a sheltered outer yacht basin, which remained until Salterns Marina was built in the early 1970s. The bomb crater entrance to the lagoon can be clearly seen.

Post-War Parkstone

berths for larger vessels were inside the inner basin. To provide weather protection along the eastern side of the pier, and so increase the number of berths, John Clark acquired a number of concrete caissons which had formed part of the Mulberry Harbour on D-Day, which were sunk in position to form an outer basin. An aerial picture shows the marina

Chapter 17 198

layout, and the recent bomb crater entrance to the lagoon.

It took John Clark a long time to realise his objective of redeveloping the Poole Harbour Yacht Club, possibly because his proposals were very ambitious. His first two planning applications were refused on appeal to the Minister. Nevertheless the yacht club itself became a great success, and throughout the 1960s and 1970s was the social heart of the area, with 1700 members, and its parties and summer balls were legend. It was predominantly a motorboat club, although it hosted a number of major international sailing events. The Committee encouraged a thriving younger section actively involved in the new sport of waterskiing; its members built a jumping ramp and laid a slalom course in what is today the 'quiet area' off Goathorn beach on the south side of the harbour.

Eventually, in 1968, John Clark got planning permission to redevelop part of the site and, a year later, sold the whole thing to the Smith family of Matchbox Toys. The Smiths sold on part of the land to an independent developer for the construction of the three blocks of flats, and designed and built the hugely successful Salterns Marina, which was opened by Sir Alec Rose in 1974.

The pre-war enthusiasm for members–only clubs continued post-war, possibly because there was little other entertainment available at that time, and there were relatively few pubs in the Parkstone area. Blake Dene House became, for a few years after the war, the Dorset Country Club, but this was not to last very long. The first plans for its redevelopment were submitted in March 1960, but it was not until 1969 that a scheme was eventually agreed with Poole's planners and the big house pulled down and it is now part of the Conifer Estate.

The successful reclamation of part of Parkstone Bay with household rubbish in the 1930s had given the Council ambitions to reclaim much more of the bay to provide much-needed public open space and a road connection between the quay and Whitecliff. An ambitious reclamation proposal was included in the Town Plan of 1952 which was reduced to 26.5 acres after strong objections from Parkstone Yacht Club and various groups of local residents. The Council went to a Public Enquiry, and the Minister eventually approved a scheme covering 43 acres which was carried out between 1961 – 1964, giving the wonderful open space we enjoy today. However, the new road never did happen.

The Blue Lagoon Club, comprising the clubhouse, swimming pool and 40 acres of tidal lagoon was put up for sale by public auction by Rebbeck Bros. of Bournemouth, on March 4th 1949. It was bought by Alderman Geoffrey Bravery, a wealthy and well respected past Mayor of Poole, who owned the 'Electric Theatres' cinema chain. He lived in a bungalow on the opposite side of Sandbanks Road and he ran the Blue Lagoon as a proprietary licensed social club. The Parkstone Unit 265 of the Sea Cadet Force had a seven year licence to moor its motor torpedo boat alongside the club wall in the lagoon, at a rent of £50 per annum.

The breach in the outer breakwater of the lagoon by the German bomb meant that the surrounding residents now looked out on to acres of mud at low tide, instead of a permanent lake with the water level controlled by the sluice gates. So they got together

261. The newly completed Salterns Marina in about 1974. The first block of flats is almost complete, but a recession in the housing market mean. that the other two blocks were completed by the mortgagee.

262. The second reclamation scheme underway in 1968, when Whitecliff was joined to Baiter and a further 43 acres of public open space and playing fields was recovered from Parkstone Bay.

with Alderman Bravery in an attempt to have the breach repaired, and hired a local man called Jack Peate to do so. His plan was to plug the gap in the breakwater with two twelve-foot steel mooring pontoons which were surplus to the requirements of the flying-boats which had, by now, returned to their peace-time base at Hythe.

263. Parkstone Bay following the reclamation of Baiter in 1960 -1964. If this is compared with the pre-war picture in Chapter 11, the extent of the new public open space becomes clear.

Peate, who was a fairly hefty lad, later described vividly how he had manoeuvred the barges into the entrance, ballasted with bags of cement, and had then gone below through a hatch to open the valves for scuttling. Unfortunately, one valve was situated beneath yet a further hatch deep in the bilge and, after opening this, he found considerable difficulty in squeezing his large frame out again. In some panic as the water gurgled in, he eventually managed to extricate himself and gradually the two pontoons sank onto the bottom of the bomb crater. However they proved totally ineffective as a barrier because they settled in a "V" formation and were quite useless as the basis for restoring the breakwater. They sat there for several years until the members of Lilliput Sailing Club took effective action.

Lilliput Sailing Club had been founded in 1956 as a 'menagerie' sailing club where, whatever the yacht, members could sail against each other on handicap. Initially the club was based in a small wooden hut at Pizey's Yard at the eastern end of Dorset Lake Avenue. This yard had previously been the Woodside Boatyard, run by Mr Knight between the wars, and before that was the house of the Works Manager for the failed industrial company, Salterns Ltd, which was sold off by the Receiver in about 1924. Within five years LSC outgrew these simple facilities, and the sheer numbers of members and their cars began to irritate Mr Pizey's neighbours, so new premises were sought. After considering, and rejecting, various possibilities, the club settled on the Blue Lagoon Club which, in 1961, was barely surviving, and was delighted to get an influx of new members joining en bloc. As well as use of the club premises, the sailors were allocated a large wooden outbuilding and a marshy and overgrown area of foreshore at the western end of the site, which they set about reclaiming as a boat park.

　　　　　　　　　　　　Post-War Parkstone

264. The Blue Lagoon Club in 1945, soon after it had been derequisitioned from its wartime use as a Services canteen and recreational facility. Alongside the outer wall of the swimming pool can be seen the Sea Cadets' training ship, Velsheda.

On arriving at the Blue Lagoon Club, LSC found that, due to the sunken pontoons blocking the new entrance, access from the harbour to the lagoon was only just possible in a dinghy at high water with the plate up; clearly a situation which had to be changed. How it was achieved is told in Alan Heron's amusing history of the club.

Initially, the removal of the pontoons had been assumed to be a simple matter, but enquires of a local contractor resulted in a quote for £3,000 to do the job, this at a time when the annual club subscription was counted in shillings rather than pounds! Fortunately, Affiliate Members of LSC included the Royal Electrical and Mechanical Engineers, and the Army Sailing Association, both based at Bovington Camp, and who kept their dinghies at the club premises. Their expertise and equipment came to the rescue in the form of a huge Scammel tank recovery vehicle from Bovington Camp. This vehicle crept along the breakwater (there being then no marina or blocks of flats to obstruct access) one Saturday in the guise of a weekend military exercise and, assisted by an eager crowd of club members, attached its recovery hawser via a two-to-one block to a bollard on the nearest pontoon. The first attempt, registering about 5O tons, tore the bollards off the deck of the pontoon, without moving it an inch. Subsequent attempts were equally unsuccessful.

Nothing deterred, work was adjourned for the day and the gallant Staff Sergeant in charge returned to Bovington for bigger blocks and more cable. Sunday saw a fresh start with a four-to-one pull. Some time later, after considerable effort, there was a mighty boiling of water and mud and the first pontoon safely slid ashore. The second pontoon was relatively easy as it slid into the gap created by the first. Lilliput Sailing Club at last had full access to the sea. Sadly the Staff Sergeant's name is nowhere recorded; the club believes it ought to be set on a tablet of stone. As it was, he and the lads who were with him seemed very happy with the club's grateful thanks and a crate of beer.

To this day the navigability of the Iagoon has always been vital to the very existence of the Club, and it remains a constant challenge. Initially it had been hoped that clearing the entrance would increase the water flow and assist in opening up a drainage channel outside. However there was no measurable effect, despite the best efforts of members who sallied forth at low tide with garden forks and spades, and a couple of tides would wipe out all trace of their work.

265. The rather gloomy interior of the Church of the Transfiguration in Chaddesley Glen, as it looked prior to its renovation in the 1960s.

At this stage the Army came to the rescue again with a proposal to lay a chain of small explosive charges as further encouragement. This was greeted with enthusiasm by the Club but proved not to be a popular idea either with the local residents, mindful of their windows, or, unsurprisingly, with the Harbour Commissioners.

The use of the Blue Lagoon Club by LSC was disrupted in 1963 by the decision of its owner, Alderman Bravery, to sell because he was moving to Jersey. He offered the premises, lock, stock and barrel to the club for £14,500, but the committee, as with all club committees, was horrified at the thought of so much money and, by the time it had got its act together, the property had been sold to some London-based property developers with ambitious plans to reclaim the whole lagoon for building houses. This was doomed to failure because Alderman Bravery had sold the freehold of the bed of the lagoon to the Harbour Commissioners ten years earlier, in April 1954 for £3,000. Poole Council granted Planning Permission for four building plots, one of which was purchased by LSC, on which they built the clubhouse which is still in use today, opened in 1966.

In 1952 the Rev. Jack Rees came to the Church of the Transfiguration as vicar. His hard work and enthusiasm, together with the steady increase in the number of parishioners, were the catalysts for the rebuilding of the "temporary" church, originally put up in 1911. In 1958, the Parochial Church Council instructed a local architect, Lionel Gregory, to draw up plans for a permanent church. His first proposal for an ultra-modern, flat-roofed building was rejected as inappropriate, but his second attempt was inspired, and resulted in the lovely church we have today.

Gregory proposed retaining the roof and structural framework of the original

building, adding extensions at the sides and ends, and then giving the whole structure a new cladding, both inside and out. The clever bit was that, by doing it in stages, worship was never interrupted during the three years of building works. First, the Sanctuary and Chancel were partitioned off from the main body of the church, and rebuilt behind a temporary screen. When this was finished, the builders took down that screen and tackled the Galilee Porch at the other end, in the same way. Finally, the side aisles were added and all the interior finishes were completed. Inside the church today, the shape of the main aisle remains the same as it always has been, and the black arches and pillars are part of the 1911 building. So is the roof, and the little dormer windows – they just have different finishes, inside and out. The new building was completed in late 1964, and consecrated by the Bishop of Salisbury on 26 May 1965.

By the mid 1960s, South Western Pottery was coming to the end of its life. Terracotta facing blocks had long since gone out of fashion, and its principal output of glazed clay drainage pipes was facing increasing competition from modern lighter plastic products. It finally closed in February 1967 and, by June 1968, Alfred Savill & Sons were offering by auction "*valuable building land of 34.39 acres with Planning Permission for 211 units of mixed residential development*". Soon Hamilton Homes were offering "*luxury new houses costing from £5695*" on Conifer Park. Jennings' Model Farm, which had become Malmesbury and Parson's Dairy, was demolished in 1958 as part of the redevelopment of Wedgewood Drive and the adjoining Edenhurst villa now lies beneath a block of flats, Dorset Lake Manor. Apart from the sensitive retention of a few street names, there is little to remind one of a century of industry and the benefits it brought to Parkstone.

So this just about brings this brief history up to date. Of the two industries which dominated the area for a hundred years each, there is little trace: the salt works is now

Kitchenham Photographers

267. The sites of South Western Pottery and Sherry & Haycock's timber yard are no longer recognisable because they are today covered with small houses, although the Cemetery can be identified centre left. Virtually all trace of industry in Parkstone-on-Sea has vanished, giving way to housing.

a muddy tidal backwater of Poole Harbour, surrounded by expensive housing; and Jennings' massive pottery is now covered by a sea of little houses. The only trace of the WWI industry at Salterns is its dock, now the marina's inner basin, but the later Harbour Club is still recognisable in the form of Salterns Hotel, recently embellished with a Blue Plaque to remind visitors of its role in the Second World War.

The original Blue Lagoon Club with its swimming pool has gone, as has the only pub in the area, the Beehive, which has been grossly over-developed with 51 retirement flats. Parkstone's most historic building, the Tudor farmhouse, Flag Farm, has been pulled down and massive modern houses and part of the golf course now cover its fields. Every conceivable square inch of those remote and peaceful sandbanks has been built on and, everywhere you look, perfectly good houses are being torn down and replaced with huge modern boxes which fetch many millions of pounds. This is now one of the most desirable residential areas on the south coast. A great deal has changed in the last two centuries, and perhaps this book will have given readers some idea of what Parkstone-on-Sea used to be like, all that time ago.

Post-War Parkstone

Index